Chocolate Fantasies

Oxmoor House®

Copyright 1987 by Oxmoor House, Inc.
Book Division of Southern Progress Corporation
P.O. Box 2463, Birmingham, Alabama 35201

Recipes adapted from *Southern Living*® cookbooks.
Southern Living® is a federally registered trademark
belonging to Southern Living, Inc.

Library of Congress Catalog Number: 87-061717

ISBN: 0-8487-0816-4

Manufactured in the United States of America

CHOCOLATE FANTASIES

Executive Editor: Ann H. Harvey
Associate Foods Editor: Margaret Chason Agnew
Editorial Assistant: Pam Beasley Bullock
Designer: Earl Freedle
Illustrator: Dwayne Coleman
Cover Photographer: Jim Bathie
Cover Stylist: Kay E. Clarke

Cover (clockwise): *Brown Sugar Fudge Cake* (Page 21), *Almond Truffles* (Page 37),
Amaretto Brownies (Page 49), and *Chocolate-Orange Mousse* (Page 59).

Contents

Introduction

Dark, rich chocolate is full of melt-in-your-mouth goodness. So what could be better than a collection of irresistible chocolate treats? From silky smooth chocolate mousse to towering chocolate cake, this sweet extravaganza is sure to be a valuable resource for lasting pleasure.

Real chocolate lovers will want to sample their way through the cookbook by starting with a mug of steaming hot chocolate accompanied by chocolate-glazed doughnuts or a wedge of chocolate cream pie. Our chocolate cakes and chocolate chip cookies will make your family and friends happy over and over again (don't be surprised if they ask for the recipes). Gift givers, knowing that chocolate candy can win the hearts of many, will delight in our luscious assortment of confections.

As an added bonus, there is an entire chapter devoted to sauces and frostings. Pick any of the rich fudge sauces and spoon them over ice cream or a slice of cake for a quick, delicious dessert. And layer cakes become showpieces with a generous spreading of our thick and creamy frostings.

We begin the book with a section of hints on how to cook with chocolate. You'll discover easy methods for melting chocolate plus simple explanations of the different types of chocolate and how they can be used interchangeably. Also included in this section are instructions for making chocolate garnishes—you'll find chocolate leaves and chocolate curls are easier to prepare than you might think.

All About Chocolate

TYPES OF CHOCOLATE

Unsweetened Chocolate: The basic chocolate from which all other products are made. It is molded into 1-ounce blocks and sold in 8-ounce packages. It may also be sold melted and packaged in envelopes.

Semisweet Chocolate: Unsweetened chocolate with sugar, extra cocoa butter, and flavorings added to give it a satiny gloss. It is molded into 1-ounce blocks and sold in 8-ounce packages or formed into chocolate chips.

Sweet Baking Chocolate (German Sweet Chocolate): Similar to semisweet chocolate, but has more sugar and is packaged in 4-ounce bars.

Milk Chocolate: Sweet chocolate with milk added. It is sold in various shapes and bars.

Almond Bark: An artificial chocolate made with vegetable fats instead of cocoa butter, with coloring and flavorings added. It is sold in 1½-pound packages or in blocks and round discs where candy supplies are sold.

Unsweetened Cocoa: A form of pure chocolate with most of the cocoa butter removed and ground into powder. It is sold in 8-ounce or 16-ounce cans.

Chocolate-Flavored Syrup: A combination of cocoa, corn syrup, and flavoring and is available in various sizes in jars, cans, or plastic containers.

CHOCOLATE SUBSTITUTIONS

We specify the type of chocolate we used in testing for each of the recipes. If you need to make substitutions, use the following information as a guide. However, for best results, always use the chocolate specified in each recipe.

To substitute for:

1 (1-ounce) square unsweetened chocolate—use 3 tablespoons unsweetened cocoa and 1 tablespoon shortening.

1 ounce semisweet chocolate—use 3 tablespoons semisweet chocolate chips or 1 (1-ounce) square unsweetened chocolate and 1 tablespoon sugar.

6-ounce package (1 cup) semisweet chocolate morsels—use 6 tablespoons unsweetened cocoa, ¼ cup sugar, and ¼ cup shortening.

4-ounce bar sweet baking chocolate—use ¼ cup unsweetened cocoa, ⅓ cup sugar, and 3 tablespoons shortening.

Note: When melted, semisweet chocolate morsels and semisweet chocolate squares can be used interchangeably.

HOW TO STORE CHOCOLATE

Store chocolate tightly wrapped or covered in a cool, dry place or in the refrigerator. If refrigerated, let it warm to room temperature before using.

Occasionally, there may be a slight graying or "bloom" on chocolate. This does not alter the quality or flavor and when used in a recipe, the chocolate will regain its color.

HOW TO MELT CHOCOLATE

Always melt chocolate with gentle heat because it scorches easily. If chocolate is to be melted alone, make certain that the container and utensils are absolutely dry; a tiny drop of moisture will cause the chocolate to become lumpy and stiff. If this should happen, stir in one teaspoon of vegetable shortening for each ounce of chocolate. Remember that unsweetened chocolate liquifies when melted, but semisweet and baking chocolate will hold their shapes until stirred. For faster melting, cut or chop chocolate into smaller pieces.

To melt chocolate, place it in a heavy saucepan over low heat and stir until melted. Or, place chocolate in top of a double boiler and melt over hot water, stirring until smooth.

To melt chocolate in a microwave oven, place a 1-ounce square in a 1-cup glass measure. Microwave, uncovered, at MEDIUM (50% power) for 1 to 2 minutes or until chocolate is almost melted. Stir until completely melted and smooth. Add 10 seconds for each additional ounce of chocolate.

To melt chocolate morsels in a microwave oven, place 1 cup chocolate morsels in a 2-cup glass measure. Microwave, uncovered, at MEDIUM (50% power) for 2 to 4 minutes or until morsels are glossy. Stir until smooth.

CHOCOLATE GARNISHES

Chocolate Leaves: Select non-poisonous leaves such as mint or rose leaves. Wash the leaves and pat dry with paper towels. Melt 1 or 2 (1-ounce) squares semisweet chocolate over hot water in a double boiler; let cool slightly. Using a small spatula, spread a thin layer of chocolate on the back of each leaf. Place leaves on a wax paper-lined cookie sheet, chocolate side up; freeze until chocolate is firm, about 10 minutes. Grasp leaf at stem end and carefully peel away from chocolate. Chill leaves until ready to use.

Chocolate Curls: Melt 4 (1-ounce) squares semisweet chocolate over hot water in a double boiler. Pour chocolate out into a wax paper-lined cookie sheet. Spread chocolate with a spatula into a 3-inch-wide strip. Smooth top with a spatula. Chill chocolate until it feels slightly tacky but not firm. (If too hard, curls will break; if too soft, chocolate will not curl.)

Gently pull a vegetable peeler across chocolate until curls form. Transfer curls to a tray by inserting a wooden pick in end of curl. Chill curls until ready to use.

Chocolate-Dipped Fruit: Make sure fruit is completely dry before dipping. Melt 4 (1-ounce) squares semisweet chocolate over hot water in a double boiler; transfer to a small bowl, and let cool slightly. Grasp fruit by stem and dip in chocolate, turning to coat the bottom of the fruit. Allow excess to drip back into bowl. Lay fruit on side on a wax paper-lined cookie sheet. Allow fruit to stand at room temperature until chocolate hardens or place in refrigerator about 10 minutes. Don't store coated fruit in refrigerator; the chocolate coating will sweat when returned to room temperature and will lose its sheen.

Chocolate Cutouts: Melt 6 (1-ounce) squares semisweet chocolate over hot water in a double boiler; cool slightly. Line a cookie sheet with aluminum foil; pour the chocolate onto the cookie sheet, and gently shake it until chocolate is smooth and level and about ⅛-inch thick. Let stand until partially set. Press a cookie cutter half-way through the chocolate to outline shapes. Remove the cutter, and let stand until chocolate is firm. When hard, reposition the cutter over the outlines, and press down to cut smoothly. Lift the cutter up, and remove the cutout by gently pressing through the cutter with a small wooden utensil (fingers will leave prints on chocolate).

Grated Chocolate: You can grate unsweetened, semisweet, or milk chocolate to sprinkle on top of pies, etc. It's easiest done in a food processor, but you can grate it by hand. When grating by hand, hold chocolate with a paper towel or wax paper so heat from your hand will not soften or melt the chocolate.

Beverages

OLD-FASHIONED HOT CHOCOLATE

- 2 (1-ounce) squares unsweetened chocolate
- 1⅓ cups boiling water
- 1 quart milk
- ⅓ cup sugar
  Pinch of salt
- ½ teaspoon vanilla extract
  Marshmallows or whipped cream (optional)

Place chocolate in top of a double boiler; bring water to a boil. Reduce heat to low; cook until chocolate melts. Gradually add 1⅓ cups boiling water, stirring constantly. Remove from heat; set aside.

Heat milk in a heavy saucepan just until thoroughly heated (do not boil). Stir in sugar and salt; add chocolate mixture, stirring well. Cook over low heat, stirring occasionally. Remove from heat; stir in vanilla. Top with marshmallows or whipped cream, if desired. Serve immediately. Yield: 6 cups.

QUICK INDIVIDUAL HOT COCOA

- 2 teaspoons cocoa
- 2 teaspoons sugar
- ¼ cup water
- ¾ cup milk
  Miniature marshmallows (optional)

Combine first 3 ingredients in a small saucepan, and bring to a boil. Boil 3 minutes, stirring constantly. Stir in milk; heat just until thoroughly heated (do not boil). Top with marshmallows, if desired. Serve immediately. Yield: 1 cup.

SPECIAL HOT CHOCOLATE

2 cups milk
½ cup candy-coated chocolate
  pieces
2 tablespoons molasses
¼ teaspoon ground ginger
  Whipped cream

Heat milk in a heavy saucepan just until thoroughly heated (do not boil). Combine candy-coated chocolate, molasses, and ginger in container of an electric blender; add milk. Process at high speed about 1 minute or until smooth. Top with whipped cream. Serve immediately. Yield: about 2½ cups.

SPICED HOT CHOCOLATE

6 cups milk
½ cup sugar
3 (1-ounce) squares unsweetened
  chocolate, cut into small pieces
1 teaspoon ground cinnamon
¼ teaspoon salt
2 eggs, beaten
2 teaspoons vanilla extract

Combine first 5 ingredients in a large saucepan, mixing well; cook over medium heat, stirring constantly, until chocolate melts. Gradually stir about one-fourth of hot mixture into eggs; add to remaining hot mixture. Cook over low heat 2 to 3 minutes, stirring constantly. Remove from heat; add vanilla, and beat at medium speed of an electric mixer until frothy. Serve immediately. Yield: 6 cups.

INSTANT COCOA-COFFEE

1 cup instant cocoa mix
⅓ cup instant coffee granules
4 cups boiling water
  Whipped cream

Combine cocoa mix, instant coffee, and boiling water; stir until coffee granules completely dissolve.
Garnish each serving with whipped cream. Serve immediately. Yield: 4 cups.

FAVORITE HOT CHOCOLATE

1½ cups sugar
½ cup cocoa
¾ teaspoon salt
5 cups water
1 (13-ounce) can evaporated milk
2 cups milk
  Marshmallows (optional)

Combine sugar, cocoa, and salt in a large Dutch oven; mix well. Slowly stir in water; bring to a boil. Add milk; cook just until thoroughly heated (do not boil).
Place marshmallows in individual cups, if desired; fill cups with hot chocolate. Serve immediately. Yield: 10 cups.

CHOCOLATE CASTLE CAPPUCCINO

3 cups cold water
¼ cup finely ground French roast
  coffee
  About ½ cup chocolate syrup
1 cup whipping cream
  Grated chocolate
5 (4-inch) sticks cinnamon

Pour water into reservoir of espresso-cappuccino maker; add coffee to filter. Brew espresso according to manufacturer's instructions, and fill coffee cups one-third full. Add 1 tablespoon plus 1 teaspoon chocolate syrup to each cup of espresso, stirring well.
Pour whipping cream into a small, deep, chilled metal or ceramic pitcher. Place steam nozzle of cappuccino maker in the bottom of the pitcher. Slowly release steam completely. Lower pitcher until end of nozzle is just below surface of cream. Continue to steam until whipping cream foams and doubles in volume. Pour foamed whipping cream over brewed espresso, filling cups full. Sprinkle each serving with grated chocolate. Place a cinnamon stick in each cup. Serve immediately. Yield: 5 cups.
Note: If steamed cream does not become frothy and double in volume, pour over espresso and stir to mix before serving.

CHOCOLATE MALT

1 cup milk
1 tablespoon plus 2 teaspoons
    chocolate malt
1½ tablespoons powdered chocolate
    flavoring for milk
1 quart vanilla ice cream, softened

Combine all ingredients in container of an electric blender; process until smooth. Pour into individual glasses. Serve immediately. Yield: 4 cups.

PLANTATION COFFEE PUNCH

1 quart chocolate milk
½ gallon chocolate, coffee, or
    vanilla ice cream, cubed and
    softened
2 quarts strong coffee, chilled
    Whipped cream
    Ground nutmeg

Combine first 3 ingredients in a punch bowl; stir until ice cream melts. Garnish with dollops of whipped cream and sprinkle with nutmeg. Yield: 20 cups.

FRENCH CHOCOLATE MILK

⅓ cup semisweet chocolate morsels
¼ cup light corn syrup
3 tablespoons water
½ teaspoon vanilla extract
1 cup whipping cream
1 quart milk, scalded

Combine chocolate morsels, corn syrup, and water in a small heavy saucepan; cook over low heat, stirring constantly, until chocolate is melted and mixture is smooth. Stir in vanilla. Cover and chill 30 to 45 minutes, stirring occasionally.

Gradually add chocolate mixture to whipping cream, beating with an electric mixer until stiff peaks form. Chill.

To serve, place ½ cup chocolate cream in each cup. Add milk, stirring well. Yield: about 7 cups.

CHOCOLATE-MINT SMOOTHIE

2 cups milk, divided
¼ cup instant cocoa mix
½ teaspoon vanilla extract
⅛ teaspoon peppermint extract
1 pint vanilla ice cream

Heat ½ cup milk in a heavy saucepan just until thoroughly heated (do not boil). Combine hot milk and cocoa mix in container of an electric blender; process until smooth. Add remaining 1½ cups milk, vanilla, and peppermint; blend well. Add ice cream, and process until mixture is smooth. Serve immediately. Yield: 4 cups.

CHOCOLATE ALEXANDERS

1 quart skim milk
2 tablespoons instant coffee powder
¼ cup chocolate syrup
½ teaspoon vanilla extract
½ to 1 teaspoon brandy extract
    Frozen whipped topping, thawed
    Grated chocolate (optional)

Combine first 3 ingredients in a heavy saucepan; cook over medium heat, stirring frequently, just until thoroughly heated (do not boil). Stir in flavorings. Ladle into mugs, and garnish with whipped topping. Sprinkle with chocolate, if desired. Serve immediately. Yield: 4 cups.

MEXICAN COFFEE

24 cups hot coffee
1 (16-ounce) can chocolate syrup
1 cup Kahlúa or other
    coffee-flavored liqueur
½ teaspoon ground cinnamon
    Whipped cream

Combine coffee, chocolate syrup, Kahlúa, and cinnamon in a large container; stir well. Top each serving with a dollop of whipped cream. Serve immediately. Yield: 25 cups.

Note: Mexican Coffee may also be served cold with a scoop of ice cream.

VIENNESE CHOCOLATE

1 (6-ounce) package semisweet
    chocolate morsels
½ cup sugar
1 teaspoon grated orange rind
⅓ cup orange juice
½ teaspoon ground cinnamon
1 cup whipping cream, whipped
    Hot milk
    Cointreau or other orange-flavored
        liqueur (optional)
    Cinnamon sticks

Combine first 5 ingredients in a heavy
saucepan. Cook over low heat, stirring
constantly, until smooth. Remove from
heat, and cool to lukewarm. Fold whipped
cream into chocolate mixture; cover and
refrigerate up to 1 week.

To serve, spoon 2 tablespoons chocolate mixture into each cup; add ⅔ cup hot
milk and 1 ounce Cointreau, if desired,
stirring until blended. Serve each with a
cinnamon stick stirrer. Yield: enough to
make about 20 cups.

FRENCH HOT CHOCOLATE

4 (1-ounce) squares unsweetened
    chocolate
¼ cup water
4 cups milk
½ cup half-and-half
½ cup sugar
2 tablespoons rum
¼ teaspoon salt
¼ teaspoon ground mace
⅛ teaspoon ground allspice
1 teaspoon vanilla extract
½ teaspoon almond extract
⅛ teaspoon ground nutmeg
½ cup whipping cream, whipped

Combine chocolate and water in a heavy
saucepan; cook over low heat, stirring
until chocolate melts. Gradually add milk,
half-and-half, sugar, rum, salt, mace, and
allspice. Cook over medium heat, stirring
with a wire whisk, until mixture is hot. Stir
in flavorings. Pour into cups. Fold nutmeg
into whipped cream. Top each cup with
whipped cream. Yield: 5 cups.

Breads

CHOCOLATE DOUGHNUTS

2 eggs
1¼ cups sugar
¼ cup vegetable oil
1 teaspoon vanilla extract
4 cups all-purpose flour
⅓ cup cocoa
1 tablespoon plus 1 teaspoon
   baking powder
1 teaspoon ground cinnamon
¾ teaspoon salt
¼ teaspoon baking soda
¾ cup buttermilk
Vegetable oil
Glaze (recipe follows)

Beat eggs at medium speed of an electric mixer until frothy. Gradually add sugar, beating until thick and lemon-colored; stir in ¼ cup vegetable oil and vanilla.

Combine the next 6 ingredients and add to egg mixture alternately with buttermilk, beginning and ending with flour mixture. Cover dough; chill several hours.

Divide dough in half. Working with one portion at a time, place dough on a lightly floured surface; roll out to ½-inch thickness. Cut dough with a floured 2½-inch doughnut cutter.

Heat 2 to 3 inches of oil to 375°; drop in 4 or 5 doughnuts at a time. Cook about 1 minute or until golden on one side; turn and cook other side about 1 minute. Drain well on paper towels. Dip each doughnut in glaze; cool on wax paper. Yield: 2 dozen.

Glaze:

4 cups sifted powdered sugar
½ teaspoon ground cinnamon
1 teaspoon vanilla extract
¼ cup plus 2 tablespoons milk

Combine all ingredients, and beat until smooth. Yield: about 2 cups.

CHOCOLATE MACAROON MUFFINS

2 cups all-purpose flour
½ cup sugar
3 tablespoons cocoa
1 tablespoon baking powder
¼ teaspoon salt
1 egg, beaten
1 cup milk
⅓ cup vegetable oil
  Macaroon Filling

Combine first 5 ingredients in a large bowl; make a well in center of mixture. Combine egg, milk, and oil; add to dry ingredients, stirring just until moistened. Spoon batter into greased muffin pans, filling one-third full. Spoon 2 teaspoons Macaroon Filling in center of each muffin cup; spoon remaining batter over top, filling each muffin cup two-thirds full. Bake at 400° for 20 minutes. Serve warm. Yield: 1 dozen.

Macaroon Filling:

1 cup flaked coconut
¼ cup sweetened condensed milk
¼ teaspoon almond extract

Combine all ingredients, mixing well. Yield: ½ cup.

CHOCOLATE APPLESAUCE BREAD

1½ cups all-purpose flour
1¼ cups sugar
1 teaspoon baking soda
¼ teaspoon baking powder
¼ teaspoon salt
½ teaspoon ground cinnamon
¼ teaspoon ground nutmeg
⅓ cup butter or margarine
2 (1-ounce) squares unsweetened
    chocolate
½ cup unsweetened applesauce
2 eggs, beaten
½ cup chopped walnuts

Combine first 7 ingredients in a large bowl, mixing well; set aside.

Melt butter and chocolate in a heavy saucepan over low heat. Add chocolate mixture, applesauce, eggs, and walnuts to flour mixture; mix well.

Pour batter into a greased and floured 9- x 5- x 3-inch loafpan. Bake at 350° for 50 to 55 minutes or until a wooden pick inserted in center comes out clean. Cool bread in pan 10 minutes; remove from pan, and cool completely on a wire rack. Yield: 1 loaf.

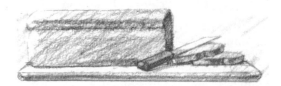

CHOCOLATE DATE-NUT BREAD

2 (1-ounce) squares unsweetened
    chocolate
1 cup hot water
1 cup chopped dates
½ cup chopped pecans or walnuts
1 teaspoon baking soda
¼ cup shortening
1 cup sugar
1 egg
2 cups all-purpose flour
½ teaspoon salt
1 teaspoon vanilla extract

Combine chocolate and water in top of a double boiler; bring water to a boil. Reduce heat to low; cook until chocolate melts. Stir in dates, pecans, and soda; cool.

Cream shortening; gradually add sugar, beating well. Add egg, and beat well.

Combine flour and salt; add to creamed mixture alternately with chocolate mixture, beginning and ending with flour mixture. Stir in vanilla.

Pour batter into 2 greased and floured 28-ounce fruit cans. Bake at 350° for 1 hour or until a wooden pick inserted in center comes out clean. Cool in cans 10 minutes; remove from cans, and cool completely. Yield: 2 loaves.

CHOCOLATE CHIP BANANA LOAF

1¾ cups all-purpose flour
¾ teaspoon baking soda
1¼ teaspoons cream of tartar
½ cup chopped walnuts
½ cup semisweet chocolate morsels
¾ cup sugar
½ cup vegetable oil
2 eggs
2 ripe bananas, sliced
½ teaspoon vanilla extract
¼ teaspoon ground cinnamon

Combine flour, soda, cream of tartar, walnuts and chocolate morsels in a large bowl; mix well, and set aside.

Combine remaining ingredients in container of an electric blender; process at medium speed 20 seconds. Stir into flour mixture, mixing well.

Pour batter into a greased 9- x 5- x 3-inch loafpan. Bake at 350° for 50 minutes or until a wooden pick inserted in center comes out clean. Cool in pan 10 minutes; remove from pan, and cool on a wire rack. Yield: 1 loaf.

CHOCOLATE-CINNAMON BUNS

1 package dry yeast
¾ cup warm water (105° to 115°)
¼ cup shortening
½ teaspoon salt
¼ cup sugar
1 egg
⅓ cup cocoa
2¼ cups all-purpose flour, divided
1 tablespoon butter or margarine, softened
3 tablespoons sugar
1½ teaspoons ground cinnamon
¾ cup sifted powdered sugar
1 tablespoon plus 1½ teaspoons milk
¼ cup chopped pecans

Dissolve yeast in warm water. Add shortening, salt, ¼ cup sugar, egg, cocoa, and 1 cup flour. Beat at medium speed of an electric mixer until smooth. Stir in

enough remaining flour to make a stiff dough. Place in a well-greased bowl, turning to grease top. Cover and let rise in a warm place (85°), free from drafts, 1 hour or until doubled in bulk.

Punch dough down. Turn dough out onto a lightly floured surface; roll into a 12- x 8-inch rectangle, and spread with butter. Combine 3 tablespoons sugar and cinnamon; sprinkle mixture over rectangle. Roll up jellyroll fashion, beginning at long side; moisten edges with water to seal. Cut rolls into 1-inch slices; place slices cut side down in a lightly greased 9-inch square baking pan. Cover; let rise in a warm place (85°), free from drafts, 1 hour or until doubled in bulk.

Bake at 375° for 20 to 25 minutes. Combine powdered sugar and milk, mixing well. Drizzle glaze over warm rolls. Sprinkle tops with pecans. Yield: 1 dozen.

CHOCOLATE STICKY BUNS

1 package dry yeast
⅓ cup warm water (105° to 115°)
⅓ cup sugar
1 teaspoon salt
½ cup butter or margarine
¾ cup milk, scalded
    About 3½ cups all-purpose flour, divided
1 egg, beaten
½ cup butter
1 cup firmly packed brown sugar
¼ cup light corn syrup
3 tablespoons cocoa
1 cup chopped pecans
1 cup sugar
2 tablespoons cocoa
2 teaspoons ground cinnamon
¼ cup butter or margarine, melted

Dissolve yeast in warm water; set aside. Combine ⅓ cup sugar, salt, ½ cup butter, and scalded milk in a mixing bowl; stir until butter melts. Cool to 105° to 115°. Stir in 1½ cups flour, egg, and yeast mixture. Beat at medium speed of an electric mixer 2½ minutes. Stir in enough remaining flour to make a soft dough.

Place dough in a greased bowl, turning to grease top. Cover and let rise in a warm place (85°), free from drafts, about 1 hour or until doubled in bulk.

Melt ½ cup butter in a small saucepan. Add brown sugar, corn syrup, and 3 tablespoons cocoa; bring to a boil and cook, stirring constantly, 1 minute. Pour sugar mixture evenly into two greased 9-inch cakepans. Sprinkle pecans over sugar mixture; set aside.

Combine 1 cup sugar, 2 tablespoons cocoa, and cinnamon; set aside.

Punch dough down, and divide in half. Roll each half into a 14- x 9-inch rectangle; brush with melted butter; sprinkle half of cocoa-cinnamon mixture over each dough rectangle. Starting at widest end, roll up each strip in jellyroll fashion; pinch edges together to seal.

Cut each roll into 1-inch slices. Place 9 slices in each cakepan. Cover and let rise in a warm place (85°), free from drafts, about 1 hour or until doubled in bulk.

Bake at 375° for 25 minutes. Invert pans on serving plates; serve warm. Yield: 1½ dozen.

COCOA-NUT SWIRL BREAD

  About 6½ cups all-purpose flour
  2 **packages dry yeast**
  1 **cup sugar, divided**
  2 **cups milk**
  ½ **cup shortening**
  1½ **teaspoons salt**
  2 **eggs**
  2 **tablespoons cocoa**
  2 **tablespoons milk**
  1 **(2½-ounce) package slivered almonds, chopped**
  Butter or margarine
  Glaze (recipe follows)

Combine 3½ cups flour and yeast in a large mixing bowl; stir well.

Combine ½ cup sugar, 2 cups milk, shortening, and salt in a small saucepan; heat until very warm (120° to 130°). Gradually add to flour mixture, stirring well. Add eggs; beat at low speed of an electric mixer 1 minute. Increase to high speed, and beat 3 minutes. Stir in enough remaining flour to make a soft dough.

Turn dough out on a lightly floured surface, and knead until smooth and elastic (about 8 to 10 minutes). Place in a well-greased bowl, turning to grease top. Cover and let rise in a warm place (85°), free from drafts, 40 to 50 minutes or until doubled in bulk.

Punch dough down, and divide in half. Turn out on a lightly floured surface. Roll each half into a 15- x 7-inch rectangle; brush each rectangle lightly with water.

Combine remaining ½ cup sugar, cocoa, and 2 tablespoons milk; mix until smooth, adding additional milk if necessary. Spread half the cocoa mixture evenly over each rectangle; sprinkle with almonds, and dot with butter. Roll up jellyroll fashion, beginning at short end. Fold ends under, and place in a greased 9- x 5- x 3-inch loafpan. Cover and let rise in a warm place (85°), free from drafts, 40 to 50 minutes, or until doubled in bulk. Bake at 375° for 30 to 35 minutes or until loaves sound hollow when tapped. Remove loaves from pans, and transfer to wire racks. Drizzle glaze over warm loaves. Yield: 2 loaves.

Glaze:

  1 **cup sifted powdered sugar**
  1½ **tablespoons milk**
  ¼ **teaspoon vanilla extract**

Combine all ingredients, mixing well. Yield: about ½ cup.

Cakes

WINNING FUDGE CAKE

3 (1-ounce) squares unsweetened chocolate
½ cup butter or margarine, softened
2¼ cups firmly packed brown sugar
3 eggs
1½ teaspoons vanilla extract
2¼ cups sifted cake flour
2 teaspoons baking soda
½ teaspoon salt
1 (8-ounce) carton commercial sour cream
1 cup boiling water
Filling (recipe follows)
Mocha Frosting
Chocolate curls (optional)
Grated chocolate (optional)

Melt chocolate in a heavy saucepan over low heat; set aside to cool. Cream butter in a large mixing bowl; gradually add sugar, beating well at medium speed of an electric mixer. Add eggs, one at a time, beating well after each addition. Add chocolate and vanilla; mix well.

Combine flour, soda, and salt; add to creamed mixture alternately with sour cream, beginning and ending with flour mixture. Stir in boiling water. (Batter will be thin.)

Pour batter into 2 greased and floured 8-inch round cakepans. Bake at 350° for 30 to 35 minutes or until a wooden pick inserted in center comes out clean. Cool in pans 10 minutes; remove from pans, and cool completely on wire racks. Split cake layers in half horizontally to make 4 layers. Spread filling between layers; spread Mocha Frosting on top and sides of cake. Refrigerate. Garnish with chocolate curls and grated chocolate, if desired. Yield: one 4-layer cake.

Filling:

1½ cups whipping cream
 1 teaspoon vanilla extract
 ½ cup sifted powdered sugar

Beat whipping cream and vanilla until foamy; gradually add powdered sugar, beating until soft peaks form. Yield: enough for one 4-layer cake.

Mocha Frosting:

 ½ cup butter or margarine, softened
 5 cups sifted powdered sugar
 ¼ cup cocoa
 ¼ cup strong coffee
 2 teaspoons vanilla extract
  About 2 tablespoons whipping
   cream

Cream butter; gradually add sugar, cocoa, coffee, and vanilla, beating at low speed of an electric mixer until light and fluffy. Add cream if too stiff, and beat well. Yield: enough for one 4-layer cake.

FAVORITE CHOCOLATE CAKE

 ½ cup shortening
 2 cups sugar
 2 eggs
 4 (1-ounce) squares unsweetened
   chocolate, melted
 2 cups sifted cake flour
 ½ teaspoon baking powder
 1 teaspoon baking soda
 1 teaspoon salt
 ¾ cup buttermilk
 ¾ cup water
 1 teaspoon vanilla extract
  Chocolate filling (recipe follows)
  Chocolate frosting
  (recipe follows)

Cream shortening; gradually add sugar, beating well at medium speed of an electric mixer. Add eggs, one at a time, beating well after each addition. Add chocolate, mixing well.

Combine flour, baking powder, soda, and salt; gradually add to the chocolate mixture alternately with buttermilk, beating well after each addition. Add water, mixing well; stir in vanilla.

Line bottom of two greased 9-inch round cakepans with wax paper. Pour batter evenly into pans; bake at 350° for 30 minutes or until a wooden pick inserted in center comes out clean.

Cool in pans 10 minutes; remove from pans and cool completely on wire racks. Peel off wax paper.

Spread chocolate filling between layers. Frost top and sides of cake with chocolate frosting. Yield: one 2-layer cake.

Chocolate Filling:

 2 tablespoons cornstarch
 ½ cup sugar
  Dash of salt
 ½ cup water
 1 tablespoon butter or margarine
 2 (1-ounce) squares semisweet
   chocolate

Combine cornstarch, sugar, salt, and water in small saucepan; cook over medium heat, stirring constantly, until thickened and bubbly. Remove from heat. Add butter and chocolate; stir until melted and smooth. Cool. Yield: enough for one 2-layer cake.

Chocolate Frosting:

 2 cups sugar
 1 cup evaporated milk
 ½ cup butter or margarine
 1 (6-ounce) package semisweet
   chocolate morsels
 1 cup marshmallow creme
 2 tablespoons milk
 1 tablespoon light corn syrup

Combine sugar, milk, and butter in a medium saucepan; cook over medium heat, stirring constantly, until mixture reaches soft ball stage (234°). Remove from heat; add chocolate, marshmallow creme, milk, and corn syrup, stirring until smooth and chocolate is melted. Cool slightly; beat until thick enough to spread. Yield: enough for one 2-layer cake.

VELVETY CHOCOLATE CAKE

½ cup buttermilk
1 teaspoon baking soda
2 cups all-purpose flour
2 cups sugar
¼ teaspoon salt
½ cup butter or margarine
1 cup water
¼ cup cocoa
2 eggs, beaten
   Velvety Chocolate Frosting

Combine buttermilk and soda. Combine flour, sugar, and salt. Combine butter, water, and cocoa in a saucepan; bring to a boil. Pour over flour mixture; cool. Add eggs and buttermilk mixture; mix well.

Pour into 2 greased and floured 8-inch round cakepans. Bake at 350° for 25 to 30 minutes or until a wooden pick inserted in center comes out clean. Cool 10 minutes; remove from pans and cool on wire racks. Spread with warm Velvety Chocolate Frosting. Yield: one 2-layer cake.

Velvety Chocolate Frosting:

½ cup butter or margarine
¼ cup plus 2 tablespoons milk
¼ cup cocoa
1 (16-ounce) package powdered
   sugar

Combine butter, milk, and cocoa in a saucepan; bring to a boil. Remove from heat; add powdered sugar, stirring well. Yield: enough for one 2-layer cake.

SOUR CREAM CHOCOLATE CAKE

4 (1-ounce) squares unsweetened
   chocolate
1 cup hot water
2 eggs, beaten
2 cups sugar
1 (8-ounce) carton commercial sour
   cream
2 teaspoons vanilla extract
2 cups all-purpose flour
1 teaspoon baking soda
½ teaspoon salt
   Frosting (recipe follows)

Combine chocolate and hot water in a small saucepan; place over low heat, stirring until chocolate melts. Remove from heat, and set aside.

Combine eggs and sugar in a medium mixing bowl, mixing well; add sour cream, chocolate mixture, and vanilla. Mix well.

Combine flour, soda, and salt; gradually add to chocolate mixture, mixing well. Pour into 2 greased and floured 8-inch round cakepans. Bake at 300° for 55 minutes or until a wooden pick inserted in center comes out clean. Cool before removing from pans. Spread frosting between layers and on top and sides of cake. Yield: one 2-layer cake.

Frosting:

2 cups sugar
¼ cup cocoa
½ cup butter or margarine
1 tablespoon light corn syrup
½ cup milk
1 cup chopped pecans
1 teaspoon vanilla extract

Combine sugar and cocoa in a small saucepan, mixing well. Add margarine, corn syrup, and milk; bring to a boil, and boil 2 minutes. Remove from heat, and cool 5 minutes. Beat at medium speed of an electric mixer until thick enough to spread. Stir in pecans and vanilla. Yield: enough for one 2-layer cake.

CHOCOLATE RUM CAKE

2 (1-ounce) squares unsweetened
   chocolate
½ cup water
½ cup butter, softened
1½ cups firmly packed light brown
   sugar
3 eggs
1¾ cups sifted cake flour
1½ teaspoons baking powder
½ teaspoon baking soda
¼ teaspoon salt
¼ cup rum
   Chocolate Rum Frosting

Grease two 9-inch cakepans; line with wax paper, and grease again. Set aside.

Combine chocolate and water in a small saucepan; place over low heat, stirring until chocolate melts. Set aside to cool.

Cream butter; gradually add sugar, beating well at medium speed of an electric mixer. Add eggs, one at a time, beating well after each addition.

Combine flour, baking powder, soda, and salt; add to creamed mixture alternately with chocolate, mixing well after each addition. Stir in rum.

Spoon batter into prepared cakepans; bake at 350° for 20 to 25 minutes or until a wooden pick inserted in center comes out clean. Cool 5 minutes in pans; remove from pans, peel off wax paper, and cool completely on wire racks.

Spread Chocolate Rum Frosting between layers and on top of cake only. Yield: one 2-layer cake.

Chocolate Rum Frosting:

    3 tablespoons semisweet chocolate
        morsels
1½ (1-ounce) squares unsweetened
        chocolate
    1 tablespoon butter or margarine
    1 cup powdered sugar
    1 egg
    2 tablespoons milk
    2 tablespoons rum

Combine chocolate and butter in top of a double boiler; bring water to a boil. Reduce heat to low; cook until chocolate melts.

Combine powdered sugar, egg, milk, and rum; mix until smooth. Stir in chocolate mixture. Place bowl in a larger bowl of ice water; beat until thick and fluffy. Yield: enough for two 9-inch layers.

BROWN SUGAR FUDGE CAKE

    ½ cup shortening
    2 cups firmly packed brown sugar
    3 eggs
    2 (1-ounce) squares unsweetened
        chocolate, melted
2¼ cups sifted cake flour
    1 teaspoon baking soda
    ½ teaspoon salt
    1 cup buttermilk
    1 teaspoon vanilla extract
        Creamy Chocolate Frosting
        Chocolate curls
        Grated semisweet chocolate

Cream shortening; gradually add sugar, beating at medium speed of an electric mixer. Add eggs, beating well after each addition. Add chocolate; beat well.

Combine flour, soda, and salt; add to creamed mixture alternately with buttermilk. Mix just until blended after each addition. Stir in vanilla.

Pour batter into 3 greased and floured 8-inch round cakepans. Bake at 350° for 25 to 30 minutes or until a wooden pick inserted in center comes out clean. Cool in pans 10 minutes; remove from pans, and cool completely on wire racks. Spread Creamy Chocolate Frosting between layers and on top and sides of cake. Garnish with chocolate curls and grated chocolate. Yield: one 3-layer cake.

Creamy Chocolate Frosting:

    ¾ cup butter or margarine
    ¾ cup cocoa
    ½ cup milk
    ¼ teaspoon salt
2¼ teaspoons vanilla extract
6¾ cups sifted powdered sugar

Combine butter, cocoa, and milk in a small saucepan; cook over low heat, stirring constantly, until butter melts. Remove from heat; add salt and vanilla. Gradually add powdered sugar, 1 cup at a time, beating at high speed of an electric mixer until thick enough to spread, adding additional milk, if necessary. Yield: enough for one 3-layer cake.

CHOCOLATE-PEANUT BUTTER CAKE

3¼ cups all-purpose flour
2¼ cups sugar
 1 tablespoon plus 1 teaspoon
    baking powder
 ½ teaspoon salt
 ½ cup butter or margarine, softened
 ½ cup creamy peanut butter
1½ cups milk
 3 eggs
1⅓ cups finely chopped unsalted
    roasted peanuts
    Chocolate-Peanut Butter Frosting
 1 (6-ounce) package semisweet
    chocolate morsels
 2 to 4 tablespoons chopped
    unsalted roasted peanuts

Combine first 4 ingredients in a large mixing bowl; mix well. Add butter, peanut butter, and milk; beat 2 minutes at medium speed of an electric mixer. Add eggs; beat 2 minutes at medium speed. Fold in 1⅓ cups chopped peanuts.

Pour batter into 3 greased and floured 9-inch round cakepans. Bake at 350° for 25 to 30 minutes or until a wooden pick inserted in center comes out clean (do not overbake). Cool in pans 10 minutes; remove layers from pans, and cool completely on wire racks.

Spread Chocolate-Peanut Butter Frosting between layers and on top and sides of cake; chill 1 hour or until firm.

Melt chocolate morsels in top of a double boiler over hot water. Drizzle around top edge and down sides of cake. Sprinkle 2 to 4 tablespoons chopped peanuts on top. Chill until ready to serve. Yield: one 3-layer cake.

Chocolate-Peanut Butter Frosting:

 1 (6-ounce) package semisweet
    chocolate morsels
 ½ cup butter or margarine, softened
 ½ cup sifted powdered sugar
1⅓ cups creamy peanut butter

Melt chocolate morsels in top of a double boiler over hot water, and set aside.

Combine remaining ingredients in a small mixing bowl; beat at medium speed of an electric mixer until smooth. Add melted chocolate to peanut butter mixture; beat until smooth. Chill 15 minutes or until thick enough to spread. Yield: enough for one 3-layer cake.

CHOCOLATE CARAMEL CAKE

 3 (1-ounce) squares unsweetened
    chocolate
 ⅔ cup butter or margarine, softened
1½ cups sugar
 ½ cup firmly packed brown sugar
 3 eggs
2⅓ cups sifted cake flour
 2 teaspoons baking soda
 ½ teaspoon salt
1⅓ cups buttermilk
 ⅓ cup water
1¼ teaspoons vanilla extract
    Caramel Filling
 ½ cup chopped pecans, divided
    Fluffy Marshmallow Frosting
 2 (1-ounce) squares unsweetened
    chocolate (optional)
    Grated chocolate (optional)

Melt 3 squares chocolate in a heavy saucepan over low heat, stirring constantly; cool slightly.

Cream butter; gradually add sugar, beating at medium speed of an electric mixer until light and fluffy. Add chocolate; mix well. Add eggs, one at a time, beating well after each addition.

Combine flour, soda, and salt; add to creamed mixture alternately with buttermilk, beginning and ending with flour mixture. Mix well after each addition. Stir in water and vanilla.

Pour batter into 3 greased and floured 9-inch round cakepans. Bake at 350° for 25 to 30 minutes or until a wooden pick inserted in center comes out clean. Cool in pans 10 minutes; remove layers from pans, and cool completely on wire racks.

Spread half of Caramel Filling on top of one layer; sprinkle with ¼ cup pecans.

Carefully spread a ½-inch-thick layer of Fluffy Marshmallow Frosting over pecans; place second cake layer on top. Repeat filling, pecan, and frosting layers; top with remaining cake layer. Spread remaining frosting over top and sides of cake.

Melt 2 squares chocolate, if desired, in a heavy saucepan over low heat, stirring constantly; cool slightly. Drizzle melted chocolate around edges and down sides of cake. Sprinkle grated chocolate over center of cake, if desired. Yield: one 3-layer cake.

Caramel Filling:

  1 cup firmly packed brown sugar
  3 tablespoons all-purpose flour
  1 cup evaporated milk
  2 egg yolks, slightly beaten
  2 tablespoons butter or margarine, softened

Combine sugar and flour in a saucepan; gradually stir in milk. Cook over medium heat, stirring constantly, until mixture thickens and boils. Boil 1 minute, stirring constantly; remove from heat. Gradually stir about one-fourth of hot mixture into yolks; add to remaining hot mixture, stirring constantly. Return to a boil and boil 1 minute, stirring constantly. Remove from heat; add butter, stirring until butter melts. Let cool. Yield: enough for two 9-inch layers.

Fluffy Marshmallow Frosting:

  2 egg whites
1½ cups sugar
  1 tablespoon plus 2 teaspoons light corn syrup
⅓ cup water
16 large marshmallows, quartered

Combine egg whites (at room temperature), sugar, corn syrup, and water in top of a double boiler; beat 1 minute at high speed of an electric mixer. Place over boiling water and beat at high speed 7 minutes. Remove from heat; transfer to a large mixing bowl. Add marshmallows; beat until spreading consistency. Yield: enough for one 3-layer cake.

BROWN MOUNTAIN CAKE

1 cup butter or margarine, softened
2 cups sugar
3 eggs
3 cups all-purpose flour
1 cup buttermilk
½ cup warm water
3 tablespoons cocoa
1 teaspoon baking soda
1 teaspoon vanilla extract
  Caramel frosting (recipe follows)
  Grated chocolate (optional)
  Pecan halves (optional)

Cream butter; gradually add sugar, beating at medium speed of an electric mixer until light and fluffy. Add eggs, one at a time, beating well after each addition. Add flour alternately with buttermilk, beginning and ending with flour. Combine water, cocoa, and soda, stirring well; slowly add to flour mixture, beating well. Stir in vanilla.

Pour batter into 2 greased and floured 9-inch round cakepans. Bake at 350° for 35 to 40 minutes or until a wooden pick inserted in center comes out clean. Cool in pans 10 minutes; remove from pans, and cool completely on wire racks.

Spread caramel frosting between layers and on top and sides of cake. Sprinkle with grated chocolate, and garnish with pecan halves, if desired. Yield: one 2-layer cake.

Caramel Frosting:

1 cup butter
2 cups sugar
1 cup evaporated milk
1 teaspoon vanilla extract

Melt butter in a heavy saucepan over medium heat; add sugar and milk. Cook mixture over medium heat, stirring constantly, until mixture reaches soft ball stage (234°). Remove from heat, and add vanilla (do not stir); cool 10 minutes.

Beat frosting at medium speed of an electric mixer about 10 minutes or until thick enough to spread. Spread immediately on cooled cake. Yield: enough for one 2-layer cake.

WHITE CHOCOLATE CAKE

¼ pound white chocolate, coarsely
    chopped
½ cup boiling water
1 cup butter or margarine, softened
2 cups sugar
4 eggs, separated
1 teaspoon vanilla extract
2½ cups sifted cake flour
1 teaspoon baking soda
1 cup buttermilk
    Coconut-Pecan Frosting

Combine chocolate and water, stirring until chocolate melts; set aside.

Cream butter; gradually add sugar, beating well at medium speed of an electric mixer. Add egg yolks, one at a time, beating well after each addition. Stir in chocolate mixture and vanilla.

Combine flour and soda; add to chocolate mixture alternately with buttermilk, beginning and ending with flour mixture. Beat egg whites (at room temperature) until stiff peaks form; fold into chocolate mixture.

Pour batter into 3 well-greased and floured 9-inch round cakepans. Bake at 350° for 25 minutes or until a wooden pick inserted in center comes out clean. Cool in pans 10 minutes; remove and cool completely on wire racks. Spread Coconut-Pecan Frosting between layers and on top and sides of cake. Yield: one 3-layer cake.

Coconut-Pecan Frosting:

1 cup evaporated milk
1½ cups sugar
¼ cup plus 2 tablespoons butter or
    margarine
4 egg yolks
1½ cups flaked coconut
1½ cups chopped pecans
1½ teaspoons vanilla extract

Combine first 4 ingredients in a heavy saucepan; bring to a boil and cook over medium heat 12 minutes, stirring constantly. Add coconut, pecans, and vanilla; stir until cool and thick enough to spread. Yield: enough for one 3-layer cake.

DARK MOCHA-CHOCOLATE CAKE

1 tablespoon butter or margarine
2 tablespoons fine, dry
    breadcrumbs
4 (1-ounce) squares unsweetened
    chocolate
½ cup water
¼ cup instant coffee granules
½ cup butter or margarine, softened
1 cup sugar
2 eggs
1¾ cups all-purpose flour
2 teaspoons baking powder
1 teaspoon ground cinnamon
¼ teaspoon ground cloves
½ cup milk
1 teaspoon vanilla extract
    Cinnamon-Cream Frosting

Grease two 8-inch round cakepans with 1 tablespoon butter; sprinkle breadcrumbs on bottom and sides of pans. Set aside.

Combine chocolate, water, and coffee granules in top of a double boiler; bring water to a boil. Reduce heat to low; cook until chocolate melts.

Cream ½ cup butter; gradually add sugar, beating well at medium speed of an electric mixer. Add eggs, one at a time, beating well after each addition. Add chocolate mixture, and beat well.

Combine flour and next 3 ingredients. Add to creamed mixture alternately with milk, beating at low speed of an electric mixer, beginning and ending with flour mixture. Do not overbeat.

Pour batter into cakepans. Bake at 350° for 20 to 25 minutes or until a wooden pick inserted in center comes out clean. Cool in pans 10 minutes; remove layers from pans, and cool completely on wire racks. Spread Cinnamon-Cream Frosting between layers and on top of cake only. Yield: one 2-layer cake.

Cinnamon-Cream Frosting:

1 cup whipping cream
2 tablespoons sugar
1 tablespoon coffee granules
¼ teaspoon ground cinnamon

Beat whipping cream until foamy; gradually add sugar, coffee granules, and cinnamon, beating until stiff peaks form. Yield: enough for two 8-inch layers.

VANILLA-FILLED CHOCOLATE CAKE

2 (1-ounce) squares unsweetened chocolate
3 tablespoons water
¾ cup butter or margarine, softened
2¼ cups sugar
4 eggs, separated
1 teaspoon vanilla extract
2¼ cups sifted cake flour
1 teaspoon cream of tartar
½ teaspoon baking soda
½ teaspoon salt
1 cup milk
   Vanilla Cream Filling
   Chocolate-Cream Cheese Frosting
¼ cup chopped almonds, toasted

Combine chocolate and water in a small saucepan; cook over low heat, stirring constantly, until chocolate melts. Cool slightly.

Cream butter; gradually add sugar, beating well at medium speed of an electric mixer. Add egg yolks, one at a time, beating well after each addition. Add chocolate mixture and vanilla; mix well.

Combine flour, cream of tartar, soda, and salt; add to creamed mixture alternately with milk, beginning and ending with flour mixture. Mix well after each addition. Beat egg whites (at room temperature) at high speed of an electric mixer until stiff peaks form; fold into batter.

Pour batter into 3 greased and floured 9-inch round cakepans; bake at 350° for 25 to 30 minutes or until a wooden pick inserted in center comes out clean. Cool in pans 10 minutes; remove from pans, and cool completely on wire racks.

Spread Vanilla Cream Filling between layers. Spread Chocolate-Cream Cheese Frosting on top and sides of cake. Sprinkle almonds over top of cake, if desired. Chill cake 3 to 4 hours before serving. Yield: one 3-layer cake.

Vanilla Cream Filling:

½ cup sugar
3 tablespoons all-purpose flour
⅛ teaspoon salt
1½ cups milk
2 eggs, beaten
¼ cup chopped almonds, toasted
½ teaspoon vanilla extract

Combine sugar, flour, and salt in a heavy saucepan; gradually stir in milk. Cook over medium heat, stirring constantly, until smooth and thickened. Gradually stir about one-fourth of hot mixture into eggs; add to remaining hot mixture, stirring constantly. Bring to a boil; cook, stirring constantly, 2 to 3 minutes or until thickened. Remove from heat; stir in almonds and vanilla. Cover and chill 1 to 2 hours. Yield: enough for one 3-layer cake.

Chocolate-Cream Cheese Frosting:

3 (1-ounce) squares unsweetened chocolate
¼ cup butter or margarine, softened
1 (8-ounce) package cream cheese, softened
3 cups sifted powdered sugar, divided
1 tablespoon plus 1 teaspoon whipping cream
   Dash of salt
½ teaspoon vanilla extract

Melt chocolate in a heavy saucepan over low heat, stirring constantly; cool.

Cream butter and cream cheese; add 1 cup powdered sugar, chocolate, whipping cream, salt, and vanilla, beating well at low speed of an electric mixer. Add remaining sugar; beat until thick enough to spread. Yield: enough for one 3-layer cake.

DOUBLE MOCHA CAKE

1 cup shortening
2½ cups sugar
5 eggs, separated
3 cups all-purpose flour
¼ cup cocoa
1 teaspoon baking soda
½ teaspoon salt
1 cup buttermilk
¼ cup plus 1 tablespoon brewed
  cold coffee
2 teaspoons vanilla extract
  Creamy Mocha Frosting
  Chocolate leaves or chocolate
  curls (optional)

Cream shortening; gradually add sugar, beating well at medium speed of an electric mixer. Beat egg yolks; add to creamed mixture, and beat well. Combine flour, cocoa, soda, and salt; add to creamed mixture alternately with buttermilk, beginning and ending with flour mixture. Stir in coffee and vanilla.

Beat egg whites (at room temperature) until stiff peaks form; fold into batter.

Pour batter into 3 greased and floured 9-inch round cakepans. Bake at 350° for 20 to 25 minutes or until a wooden pick inserted in center comes out clean. Cool in pans 10 minutes; remove layers from pans, and cool completely on wire racks. Spread Creamy Mocha Frosting between layers and on top and sides of cake. Garnish with chocolate leaves, if desired. Yield: one 3-layer cake.

Creamy Mocha Frosting:

¾ cup butter or margarine, softened
6 cups sifted powdered sugar
1 tablespoon cocoa
1 egg yolk, beaten
¼ cup plus 1½ teaspoons brewed
  cold coffee
1½ teaspoons vanilla extract

Cream butter. Combine powdered sugar and cocoa; gradually add to butter, beating at low speed of an electric mixer until smooth. Add remaining ingredients, and beat until frosting is light and fluffy. Yield: enough for one 3-layer cake.

BELGIAN MOCHA CAKE

½ cup sugar
3 tablespoons water
2 (1-ounce) squares unsweetened
  chocolate
¾ cup butter or margarine, softened
2 cups sugar
1 teaspoon vanilla extract
4 eggs, separated
2¼ cups cake flour
½ teaspoon baking soda
½ teaspoon salt
1 cup milk
1 teaspoon cream of tartar
  Mocha frosting (recipe follows)
  Chocolate curls or grated
  chocolate (optional)

Combine ½ cup sugar, water, and chocolate in a heavy saucepan; cook over low heat, stirring until chocolate melts. Remove from heat; cool.

Cream butter; gradually add sugar, beating well at medium speed of an electric mixer. Stir in vanilla. Add egg yolks, one at a time, beating well after each addition. Stir in chocolate mixture.

Combine flour, soda, and salt; add to creamed mixture alternately with milk, beginning and ending with flour mixture. Mix well after each addition. Beat egg whites (at room temperature) at high speed of an electric mixer until frothy; add cream of tartar, and beat until stiff peaks form. Fold into batter.

Grease three 9-inch round cakepans; line with wax paper; grease again and dust with flour. Pour batter into pans; bake at 350° for 25 to 30 minutes or until a wooden pick inserted in center comes out clean. Remove layers; cool on wire racks.

Spread mocha frosting between layers and on top and sides of cake. Store in refrigerator. Garnish with chocolate curls, if desired. Yield: one 3-layer cake.

Mocha Frosting:

1 cup butter, softened
2 to 2¼ cups powdered sugar,
    divided
1 tablespoon instant coffee granules
¾ teaspoon cocoa
¾ teaspoon hot water
2 egg yolks
1 to 1½ tablespoons almond extract
2 tablespoons rum

Cream butter and 1½ cups powdered sugar, beating at low speed of an electric mixer until light and fluffy. Combine coffee granules, cocoa, and water; stir into creamed mixture. Add egg yolks, and beat 5 minutes. Stir in almond extract and rum. Add enough of remaining sugar to make thick enough to spread (frosting gets quite firm when refrigerated). Yield: enough for one 3-layer cake.

CHOCOLATE VELVET TORTE

8 (1-ounce) squares sweet baking
    chocolate
¾ cup butter or margarine
¼ cup plus 2 tablespoons
    all-purpose flour
6 eggs, separated
½ cup sugar
⅔ cup raspberry preserves
    Chocolate glaze (recipe follows)

Combine chocolate and butter in a heavy saucepan; cook over low heat until melted, stirring often. Remove from heat, and stir in flour. Add egg yolks, one at a time, stirring well after each addition; set aside.

Beat egg whites (at room temperature) at high speed of an electric mixer until foamy; gradually add sugar, 1 tablespoon at a time, beating until stiff peaks form and sugar dissolves.

Fold egg whites into chocolate mixture. Pour into 3 greased and floured 8-inch round cakepans; bake at 350° for 20 to 25 minutes or until a wooden pick inserted in center comes out clean. Cool in pans 10 minutes (layers settle as they cool). Remove layers; cool on wire racks.

Spread ⅓ cup raspberry preserves between each layer; drizzle chocolate glaze on top. Yield: one 3-layer torte.

Chocolate Glaze:

4 (1-ounce) squares sweet baking
    chocolate
2 tablespoons water
3 tablespoons butter or margarine,
    softened

Combine chocolate and water in a heavy saucepan; cook over low heat until melted, stirring often. Remove from heat; stir in butter. Cool until desired consistency, stirring occasionally. Yield: enough for one 3-layer torte.

MOCHA BROWNIE TORTE

1 (15.5-ounce) package fudge
    brownie mix
2 eggs, beaten
2 tablespoons water
½ cup chopped pecans
1 cup whipping cream
3 tablespoons plus 1 teaspoon
    brown sugar
2 teaspoons instant coffee granules
    Additional flavored whipped
        cream for piping (optional)
    Shaved chocolate (optional)
    Chocolate curls (optional)

Lightly grease two 8-inch round cakepans; line with wax paper, and grease again. Set aside.

Combine brownie mix, eggs, and water; mix well. Stir in pecans. Spread batter in pans. Bake at 350° for 15 to 18 minutes. Cool 5 minutes; remove layers from pans, and cool completely on wire racks.

Beat whipping cream until foamy; gradually add sugar and coffee granules, beating until stiff peaks form.

Spread whipped cream mixture between layers and on top and sides of cake. Garnish with piped whipped cream mixture, shaved chocolate, and chocolate curls, if desired. Chill until serving time. Yield: one 2-layer torte.

CHOCOLATE CHIP-SOUR CREAM CAKE

½ cup butter or margarine, softened
1 cup sugar
2 eggs
2 cups all-purpose flour
1 teaspoon baking powder
1 teaspoon baking soda
1 (8-ounce) carton commercial sour
    cream
1 teaspoon vanilla extract
1 (6-ounce) package semisweet
    chocolate morsels
1 cup chopped pecans
¼ cup firmly packed brown sugar

Cream butter; gradually add 1 cup sugar, beating at medium speed of an electric mixer until light and fluffy. Add eggs, one at a time, beating well.

Combine flour, baking powder, and soda; add one-third of dry ingredients to creamed mixture, stirring with a spoon until blended. Add half of sour cream, stirring until blended. Repeat procedure, ending with flour mixture. Stir in vanilla.

Combine chocolate morsels, pecans, and brown sugar; set aside.

Spoon half of batter into a well-greased and floured 10-inch tube pan. Sprinkle with half of chocolate morsel mixture. Spoon remaining batter into pan, and top with remaining chocolate morsel mixture. Bake at 350° for 50 minutes or until a wooden pick inserted in center comes out clean. Remove from pan, and cool completely. Yield: one 10-inch cake.

ROCKY ROAD CAKE

1 (27¼-ounce) package chocolate
    macaroon ring cake mix
1¼ cups water
¼ cup butter or margarine, softened
2 eggs
½ cup miniature marshmallows
½ cup finely chopped pecans
1 (6-ounce) package semisweet
    chocolate morsels, divided
⅓ cup water
1 tablespoon plus 1 teaspoon water

The package of cake mix should include separate envelopes: cake mix, macaroon mixture, and glaze mix.

Combine cake mix, 1¼ cups water, butter, and eggs in a large mixing bowl; beat 2 minutes at highest speed of an electric mixer. Stir in marshmallows, pecans and ½ cup chocolate morsels. Spoon batter into a greased and floured 10-inch Bundt pan or tube pan.

Combine macaroon mix, ⅓ cup water, and remaining chocolate morsels; mix well. Spoon over chocolate batter without touching sides of pan.

Bake at 350° for 40 to 45 minutes or until a wooden pick inserted in center comes out clean. Cool 25 minutes; remove from pan, and cool on a wire rack.

Combine glaze mix and 1 tablespoon plus 1 teaspoon water; mix until smooth. Spoon over cake. Yield: one 10-inch cake.

CHOCOLATE SPONGE CAKE

2 cups superfine sugar
¾ cup all-purpose flour
½ cup cocoa
12 egg whites
1 teaspoon cream of tartar
1 teaspoon vanilla extract

Sift sugar, flour, and cocoa together; set aside.

Beat egg whites (at room temperature) at high high speed of an electric mixer until foamy. Add cream of tartar and vanilla; beat 5 minutes or until stiff peaks form.

Sprinkle one-fourth of flour mixture over egg whites; gently fold in with a rubber spatula. Repeat procedure with remaining flour mixture, adding one-fourth of the mixture at a time. Spoon into an ungreased 10-inch tube pan with removable bottom. Bake at 375° for 40 minutes or until cake springs back when touched lightly with fingers. Invert pan on funnel or bottle for 2 hours or until cake is completely cooled.

Loosen cake from sides of tube pan, using a small metal spatula; gently remove from pan. Yield: one 10-inch cake.

HOLIDAY LOG CAKE

¾ teaspoon baking powder
¼ teaspoon salt
4 eggs
¾ cup sugar
¾ cup all-purpose flour
¼ cup cocoa
1 teaspoon vanilla extract
2 to 3 tablespoons powdered sugar
2 cups sweetened whipped cream
3 (1-ounce) squares unsweetened
  chocolate
¼ cup butter or margarine
1 tablespoon instant coffee granules
  Dash of salt
⅓ cup boiling water
  About 2½ cups powdered sugar
  Candied cherries

Lightly grease a 15- x 10- x 1-inch jellyroll pan; line with wax paper, and grease lightly. Set aside.

Combine baking powder, ¼ teaspoon salt, and eggs (at room temperature) in mixing bowl; beat at medium speed of an electric mixer until blended. Gradually add sugar, beating until thick and lemon colored. Fold in flour, cocoa, and vanilla.

Spread mixture evenly into prepared pan. Bake at 400° for 13 minutes or until surface springs back when gently pressed.

Sift 2 to 3 tablespoons powdered sugar in a 15- x 10-inch rectangle on a linen towel. Turn cake out on sugar; remove wax paper from cake. Trim edges, if necessary. Starting with short end, roll up cake and towel, jellyroll fashion. Cool thoroughly on wire rack. Unroll; spread with whipped cream, and reroll. Chill.

Place chocolate in top of a double boiler; bring water to a boil. Reduce heat to low; cook until chocolate melts. Blend in butter, coffee, dash of salt, and boiling water, stirring until smooth. Cool to lukewarm. Stir in about 2½ cups powdered sugar to make a spreading consistency.

Spread frosting evenly over cake. Mark frosting with tines of a fork to resemble bark of a tree and decorate with candied cherries. Refrigerate until serving time. Yield 8 to 10 servings.

ROLLED CHOCOLATE ICE CREAM CAKE

½ cup all-purpose flour
⅓ cup cocoa
1 teaspoon baking powder
¼ teaspoon salt
4 eggs, separated
¾ cup sugar
½ teaspoon vanilla extract
¼ teaspoon almond extract
1 quart vanilla ice cream, softened
  Chocolate frosting (recipe
    follows)
  Chopped dry-roasted pistachios
  Whole dry-roasted pistachios

Grease a 15- x 10- x 1-inch jellyroll pan. Line with wax paper; grease again. Sift first 4 ingredients together; set aside.

Beat egg whites (at room temperature) at high speed of an electric mixer until foamy. Gradually add sugar, beating until soft peaks form; set aside.

Beat egg yolks until thick and lemon colored; stir in flavorings. Fold yolk mixture into egg white mixture; then gently fold in flour mixture. Spread evenly in prepared pan. Bake at 350° for 12 minutes.

When cake is done, immediately loosen from sides of pan and turn out onto a damp towel. Peel off wax paper. Starting at wide end, roll up cake and towel together; cool 30 minutes on wire rack, seam side down.

Unroll cake; remove towel. Spread ice cream over cake. Gently roll cake back up; place on a large baking sheet, seam side down. Freeze until ice cream is firm.

Frost cake with chocolate frosting; freeze until serving time. Sprinkle with pistachios. Yield: 8 to 10 servings.

Chocolate Frosting:

¼ cup butter or margarine, softened
3 tablespoons milk
3 tablespoons cocoa
2 cups sifted powdered sugar
1 teaspoon vanilla extract

Combine all ingredients; beat until smooth. Yield: enough frosting for one cake roll.

CHOCOLATE CHIP
COFFEE CAKE

1 cup butter or margarine, softened
1 cup sugar
3 eggs
3 cups all-purpose flour
1 tablespoon baking powder
1 teaspoon baking soda
½ teaspoon salt
1 (8-ounce) carton commercial sour
   cream
1 (12-ounce) package semisweet
   chocolate morsels
½ cup firmly packed brown sugar
1 teaspoon ground cinnamon

Cream butter; gradually add sugar, beating at medium speed of an electric mixer until light and fluffy. Add eggs, one at a time, beating well after each addition.

Combine flour, baking powder, soda, and salt; add to creamed mixture alternately with sour cream, beginning and ending with flour mixture. Spoon half of batter into a greased and floured 13- x 9- x 2-inch baking pan.

Combine chocolate morsels, brown sugar, and cinnamon; sprinkle 1½ cups of chocolate morsel mixture over batter. Top with remaining batter. Sprinkle with remaining chocolate morsel mixture. Bake at 350° for 35 to 40 minutes. Serve warm or at room temperature. Yield: 15 to 18 servings.

BUTTERMILK CHOCOLATE CAKE

2 cups all-purpose flour
2 cups sugar
1 teaspoon baking soda
1 cup water
½ cup butter or margarine
¼ cup cocoa
2 eggs
½ cup buttermilk
   Coconut Chocolate Frosting

Combine flour, sugar, and soda in a large mixing bowl. Combine water, butter, and cocoa in a small saucepan; cook over low heat until mixture comes to a boil;

remove from heat and pour over dry ingredients, mixing thoroughly. Add eggs and buttermilk; beat well.

Spoon batter into a well-greased 13- x 9- x 2-inch baking pan. Bake at 350° for 30 minutes or until a wooden pick inserted in center comes out clean. Cool in pan. Frost with Coconut Chocolate Frosting. Yield: 15 to 18 servings.

Coconut Chocolate Frosting:

1 (16-ounce) package powdered
   sugar
1 cup chopped pecans
1 cup shredded coconut
⅓ cup plus 2 teaspoons milk
½ cup butter or margarine
3 tablespoons cocoa

Combine powdered sugar, pecans, and coconut in a large mixing bowl; set aside. Combine milk, butter, and cocoa in a small saucepan; cook over low heat, stirring until mixture comes to a boil. Add chocolate mixture to sugar mixture; beat with an electric mixer until frosting is fluffy. Yield: enough for one 13- x 9- x 2-inch cake.

CHOCOLATE CANDY CAKE

2 cups all-purpose flour
2 cups sugar
1 teaspoon baking soda
1 cup water
1 cup butter or margarine
¼ cup cocoa
½ cup buttermilk
2 eggs, slightly beaten
1 teaspoon vanilla extract
   Chocolate Candy Frosting

Combine flour, sugar, and soda; mix well, and set aside.

Combine water, butter, and cocoa in a heavy saucepan; bring to a boil, stirring constantly. Stir into flour mixture; add buttermilk, eggs, and vanilla. Pour into a greased and floured 13- x 9- x 2-inch baking pan. Bake at 350° for 30 minutes or until a wooden pick inserted in center comes out clean. Prick cake at 1-inch intervals with a fork; spread with Chocolate Candy Frosting. Yield: 15 servings.

Chocolate Candy Frosting:

½ cup butter or margarine
¼ cup plus 2 tablespoons
    evaporated milk
¼ cup cocoa
1 (16-ounce) package powdered
    sugar, sifted
1 teaspoon vanilla extract
½ cup chopped pecans or walnuts

Combine butter, milk, and cocoa in a heavy saucepan; bring to a boil, stirring constantly. Stir in sugar; return to a boil, stirring constantly. Immediately remove from heat. Add vanilla and pecans; stir constantly 3 to 5 minutes or until frosting begins to lose its gloss. Yield: enough for one 13- x 9- x 2-inch cake.

FUDGY PEANUT BUTTER CAKE

2 cups all-purpose flour
2 cups sugar
1 teaspoon baking soda
1 cup water
1 cup butter or margarine
¼ cup cocoa
½ cup buttermilk
2 eggs, slightly beaten
1 teaspoon vanilla extract
1 cup creamy peanut butter
1 tablespoon vegetable oil
¼ cup plus 1 tablespoon butter or
    margarine
3 tablespoons cocoa
¾ teaspoon vanilla extract
3 to 5 tablespoons buttermilk
2½ cups sifted powdered sugar

Combine flour, sugar, and soda; mix well, and set aside.

Combine water, 1 cup butter, and ¼ cup cocoa in a heavy saucepan; bring to a boil, stirring constantly. Gradually stir into flour mixture. Stir in ½ cup buttermilk, eggs, and 1 teaspoon vanilla. Pour into a greased and floured 13- x 9- x 2-inch baking pan; bake at 350° for 30 minutes or until a wooden pick inserted in center comes out clean. Cool in pan.

Combine peanut butter and oil; mix well. Spread on cooled cake.

Combine ¼ cup plus 1 tablespoon butter and 3 tablespoons cocoa in a small saucepan; cook over low heat, stirring constantly, until butter melts and mixture is smooth. Remove from heat; add remaining ingredients. Beat until thick enough to spread; spread over peanut butter mixture. Yield: 15 servings.

CHOCOLATE-NUT CUPCAKES

⅓ cup shortening
1 cup sugar
1 egg
2 cups all-purpose flour
½ teaspoon salt
2½ teaspoons baking powder
¾ cup milk
1 teaspoon vanilla extract
1 (6-ounce) package semisweet
    chocolate morsels
½ cup chopped walnuts
1 (16½-ounce) can milk chocolate
    frosting

Cream shortening; gradually add sugar, beating at medium speed of an electric mixer until light and fluffy. Add egg, beating well. Combine flour, salt, and baking powder; add to creamed mixture, and mix well. Add milk, vanilla, chocolate morsels, and nuts; mix well.

Spoon batter into lightly greased muffin pans, filling two-thirds full. Bake at 375° for 20 minutes. Remove from pan; cool completely. Frost with chocolate frosting. Yield: 1½ dozen.

MARBLE CHOCOLATE CHIP CUPCAKES

1 (8-ounce) package cream cheese, softened
1½ cups sugar, divided
1 egg, slightly beaten
⅛ teaspoon salt
1 (6-ounce) package semisweet chocolate morsels
1½ cups all-purpose flour
1 teaspoon baking soda
½ teaspoon salt
¼ cup cocoa
1 cup water
½ cup vegetable oil
1 tablespoon vinegar
1 teaspoon vanilla extract

Combine cream cheese and ½ cup sugar; beat until smooth. Add egg, ⅛ teaspoon salt, and chocolate morsels, stirring well. Set aside.

Combine flour, remaining 1 cup sugar, soda, ½ teaspoon salt, and cocoa; stir until blended. Add water, oil, vinegar, and vanilla; stir until batter is smooth. Spoon batter into paper-lined muffin pans, filling half full. Spoon a tablespoonful of cream cheese mixture into center of each cupcake. Bake at 350° for 25 to 30 minutes or until done. Remove from pan; cool. Yield: 1½ dozen cupcakes.

CHOCOLATE CHIP CHEESECAKE

1 cup vanilla wafer crumbs
¼ cup butter, melted
2 (8-ounce) packages cream cheese, softened
¾ cup sugar
1 (8-ounce) carton commercial sour cream, divided
4 eggs
1 teaspoon vanilla extract
1 (6-ounce) package semisweet chocolate morsels
½ cup sugar
1½ teaspoons lemon juice
1½ teaspoons vanilla extract
Additional semisweet chocolate morsels (optional)

Combine wafer crumbs and butter, mixing well. Press mixture into bottom of a 9-inch springform pan; set aside.

Beat cream cheese at low speed of an electric mixer until light and fluffy; gradually add ¾ cup sugar and ½ cup sour cream, mixing well. Add eggs, one at a time, beating well after each addition. Stir in 1 teaspoon vanilla and 1 package chocolate morsels. Spoon into prepared pan. Bake at 325° for 1 hour. Cool at room temperature on a wire rack for 20 minutes.

Combine remaining sour cream, ½ cup sugar, lemon juice, and 1½ teaspoons vanilla, mixing well; gently spread over top of cheesecake. Bake at 475° for 5 minutes. Cool to room temperature on a wire rack; refrigerate 8 hours. Remove sides of springform pan; sprinkle additional chocolate morsels around top edge and in center of cheesecake, if desired. Yield: one 9-inch cheesecake.

MARBLE MINT CHEESECAKE

3 tablespoons graham cracker crumbs
1 (16-ounce) carton cream-style cottage cheese
2 (8-ounce) packages cream cheese, softened
1½ cups sugar
4 eggs, slightly beaten
1 (16-ounce) carton commercial sour cream
½ cup butter, melted
⅓ cup cornstarch
¾ teaspoon peppermint extract
8 (1-ounce) squares semisweet chocolate
1 (8-ounce) carton frozen whipped topping, thawed
1 (8-ounce) jar chocolate fudge topping
2 tablespoons crème de menthe syrup

Grease a 9-inch springform pan. Coat bottom and sides of pan with graham cracker crumbs, and set aside.

Place cottage cheese in container of electric blender, and process until smooth;

set aside. Beat cream cheese at low speed of an electric mixer until smooth; add cottage cheese, sugar, and eggs, beating well. Add next 4 ingredients, beating at low speed of electric mixer.

Place chocolate in top of double boiler; bring water to a boil. Reduce heat to low; cook until chocolate melts. Remove from heat, and add 1½ cups of cream cheese mixture; blend thoroughly.

Pour half of remaining cream cheese mixture into prepared pan, and top with half of chocolate mixture. Repeat layers. Gently cut through batter in zigzag fashion in several places. Bake at 325° for 1 hour and 15 to 20 minutes. Turn oven off, and allow cheesecake to cool in oven for 2 hours. Remove; cool to room temperature on a wire rack. Chill several hours.

Remove sides of springform pan. Pipe whipped topping over top of cheesecake. Combine chocolate topping and créme de menthe syrup. To serve, drizzle chocolate topping mixture over each slice. Yield: one 9-inch cheesecake.

BLACK FOREST CHEESECAKE

1½ cups chocolate wafer crumbs
¼ cup butter or margarine, melted
3 (8-ounce) packages cream cheese, softened
1½ cups sugar
4 eggs
⅓ cup kirsch or other cherry-flavored liqueur
4 (1-ounce) squares semisweet chocolate
½ cup commercial sour cream
  Whipped cream
  Maraschino cherries with stems

Combine chocolate wafer crumbs and butter, mixing well; firmly press into bottom and 1 inch up sides of a 9-inch springform pan.

Beat cream cheese at low speed of an electric mixer until light and fluffy; gradually add sugar, mixing well. Add eggs, one at a time, beating well after each addition. Stir in kirsch, and mix until blended. Pour into prepared pan. Bake at 350° for 1 hour.

Cool to room temperature on a wire rack.

Place chocolate in top of a double boiler; bring water to a boil. Reduce heat to low; cook until chocolate melts. Cool slightly. Stir in sour cream. Spread chocolate mixture evenly over top. Chill thoroughly. Garnish with whipped cream and cherries. Yield: one 9-inch cheesecake.

RICH CHOCOLATE CHEESECAKE

1½ cups chocolate wafer crumbs
¼ teaspoon ground nutmeg
½ cup butter, melted
2 (8-ounce) packages cream cheese, softened
¾ cup sugar
3 eggs
1 (8-ounce) carton commercial sour cream
6 (1-ounce) squares semisweet chocolate, melted
1 tablespoon plus ¾ teaspoon cocoa
1½ teaspoons vanilla extract
½ cup whipping cream, whipped
  Additional whipped cream (optional)
  Chocolate curls (optional)
  Almonds (optional)
  Maraschino cherries (optional)

Combine first 3 ingredients, mixing well. Press mixture into bottom of a 9-inch springform pan; chill.

Beat cream cheese at low speed of an electric mixer until light and fluffy; gradually add sugar, mixing well. Add eggs, one at a time, beating well after each addition. Stir in sour cream, melted chocolate, cocoa, and vanilla; mix well. Gently fold in whipped cream; spoon into prepared pan.

Bake at 300° for 1 hour. Turn oven off; allow cheesecake to cool in oven 30 minutes. Open door, and allow cheesecake to cool in oven an additional 30 minutes. Refrigerate 8 hours. Remove sides of springform pan, and garnish with additional whipped cream, chocolate curls, almonds, and cherries, if desired. Yield: one 9-inch cheesecake.

Candies

CREAMY PECAN FUDGE

3 (12-ounce) packages semisweet
   chocolate morsels
1 (7-ounce) jar marshmallow creme
1 cup butter or margarine
4½ cups sugar
1 (13-ounce) can evaporated milk
3 to 4 cups chopped pecans

Combine chocolate morsels, marshmallow creme, and butter; set aside.

Combine sugar and evaporated milk in a heavy saucepan; bring to a boil. Reduce heat to low and cook 9 minutes, stirring constantly. Pour over chocolate morsel mixture, stirring until chocolate melts and mixture is smooth. Add pecans; stir until well blended.

Spread mixture in a lightly buttered 15- x 10- x 1-inch jellyroll pan. Chill until firm and cut into squares. Cover and store in refrigerator. Yield: 10 dozen.

CREAM CHEESE FUDGE

4 (1-ounce) squares unsweetened
   chocolate
2 (3-ounce) packages cream cheese,
   softened
4 cups sifted powdered sugar
½ teaspoon vanilla extract
1 cup chopped pecans or walnuts
   Pecan halves

Place chocolate in top of a double boiler; bring water to a boil. Reduce heat to low; cook until chocolate melts.

Combine cream cheese and sugar, beating at low speed of an electric mixer until smooth. Add melted chocolate and vanilla, beating well. Stir in chopped pecans. Press mixture into a lightly greased 8-inch square pan. Chill until firm and cut into squares. Top each square with a pecan half. Store fudge in refrigerator. Yield: about 1½ dozen.

CHOCOLATE-CARAMEL FUDGE

3 cups firmly packed light brown
  sugar
3 tablespoons all-purpose flour
1½ cups molasses
¾ cup butter or margarine
6 (1-ounce) squares unsweetened
  chocolate
1½ cups milk
1½ teaspoons vanilla extract
⅓ cup sliced almonds, toasted

Combine first 4 ingredients in a heavy saucepan. Bring to a boil, stirring constantly; reduce heat, and cook 5 minutes. Add chocolate and milk; stir until chocolate melts. Cook over medium heat, stirring frequently, until mixture reaches soft ball stage (234°). Remove from heat, and stir in vanilla.

Pour mixture into a buttered 9-inch square pan; sprinkle with almonds. Cover and chill overnight; cut into squares. Store in refrigerator. Yield: 3 dozen.

PISTACHIO FUDGE

4 cups sugar
2 cups milk
½ cup butter or margarine
¼ teaspoon salt
1 teaspoon vanilla extract
¼ cup finely chopped dry-roasted
  pistachios
  Candied red and green cherries

Combine first 4 ingredients in a large Dutch oven. Cook over low heat, stirring constantly, until sugar dissolves. Increase to medium heat and cook, stirring occasionally, until mixture reaches soft ball stage (234°). Remove from heat (do not stir). Cool to lukewarm (110°).

Add vanilla and pistachios; beat with a wooden spoon for 2 to 3 minutes or until mixture is thick and begins to lose its gloss. Pour into a buttered 8-inch square pan. Mark top of warm fudge into 1⅓-inch squares. Decorate each square with candied cherries. Cool and cut into squares. Yield: 3 dozen.

CHERRY-NUT FUDGE

3⅔ cups sifted powdered sugar
½ cup cocoa
½ cup butter or margarine
3 tablespoons milk
1 tablespoon vanilla extract
½ cup chopped candied cherries
½ cup chopped pecans

Combine powdered sugar and cocoa; stir well. Set aside.

Combine butter and milk in a medium saucepan; cook over low heat until butter melts. Remove from heat, and stir in cocoa mixture until smooth. Add vanilla, cherries, and pecans; stir well. Pour mixture into a lightly greased 8-inch square pan; chill until firm. Cut into squares. Yield: about 2½ dozen.

DOUBLE PEANUT FUDGE

2 cups sugar
⅔ cup milk
1 cup marshmallow creme
1 cup creamy peanut butter
1 (6-ounce) package semisweet
  chocolate morsels
1 teaspoon vanilla extract
½ cup coarsely chopped peanuts

Combine sugar and milk in a heavy saucepan. Cook over medium heat, stirring occasionally, until mixture reaches soft ball stage (234°). Remove from heat; add next 4 ingredients. Stir until mixture is well blended; fold in peanuts. Pour into a buttered 8-inch square pan. Cool and cut into squares. Yield: 3 dozen.

FUDGE SCOTCH RING

1 cup walnut halves
1 (6-ounce) package semisweet
   chocolate morsels
1 (6-ounce) package butterscotch
   morsels
1 (14-ounce) can sweetened
   condensed milk
1 cup coarsely chopped walnuts
½ teaspoon vanilla extract
   Red and green candied cherries

Line bottom of a 9-inch pieplate with a 12-inch square of aluminum foil. Place a custard cup in center of pieplate. Arrange 1 cup walnut halves around custard cup, forming a 2-inch wide ring; set aside.

Combine chocolate morsels, butterscotch morsels, and condensed milk in top of a double boiler; bring water to a boil. Reduce heat to low, and cook, stirring occasionally, until morsels melt and mixture begins to thicken and become smooth. Remove from heat; stir in 1 cup chopped walnuts and vanilla. Chill 1 hour.

Spoon chocolate-butterscotch mixture in mounds over walnut halves; remove custard cup. Decorate with candied cherries. Yield: one 8-inch ring.

ROCKY ROAD FUDGE

1 (12-ounce) package semisweet
   chocolate morsels
1 (14-ounce) can sweetened
   condensed milk
2 tablespoons butter or margarine
2 cups dry-roasted peanuts
1 (10½-ounce) package miniature
   marshmallows

Place chocolate morsels, milk, and butter in top of a double boiler; bring to a boil. Reduce heat to low; cook until chocolate and butter melt, stirring constantly. Remove from heat, and stir in peanuts and marshmallows. Spread mixture into a wax paper-lined 13- x 9- x 2-inch baking pan. Chill at least 2 hours. Cut into 1½-inch squares. Store in refrigerator. Yield: about 4 dozen.

CHOCOLATE FUDGE

2½ cups sugar
1 (5.33-ounce) can evaporated milk
2 (1-ounce) squares unsweetened
   chocolate
2 tablespoons light corn syrup
   Dash of salt
2 tablespoons butter
1 teaspoon vanilla extract
1 cup chopped pecans or walnuts

Combine first 5 ingredients in a Dutch oven. Cook over low heat, stirring constantly, until sugar dissolves.

Continue to cook, stirring often until mixture reaches soft ball stage (234°). Remove from heat; add butter and vanilla (do not stir). Cool to lukewarm (110°).

Add pecans; beat with a wooden spoon until mixture is thick and begins to lose its gloss (2 to 3 minutes). Pour into a buttered 8-inch square pan. Mark warm fudge into 1⅓-inch squares. Cool and cut into squares. Yield: 3 dozen.

CHOCOLATE-NUT FUDGE LOG

1⅓ cups sugar
¼ teaspoon salt
2 tablespoons cocoa
¾ cup milk
1 tablespoon light corn syrup
2 tablespoons butter or margarine
1 teaspoon vanilla extract
½ cup finely chopped pecans

Combine sugar, salt, and cocoa in a heavy saucepan; mix well. Gradually stir in milk and syrup. Cook over medium heat, stirring occasionally, until mixture reaches soft ball stage (234°). Remove from heat; stir in butter and vanilla. Pour into a buttered 15- x 10- x 1-inch jellyroll pan; cool 10 minutes.

With buttered hands, knead candy occasionally for 10 to 15 minutes or until cool enough to hold its form. Shape into a 12- x 1¼-inch rope; roll in pecans. wrap in buttered plastic wrap. Cool at room temperature for 1 hour or until completely cooled. Cut into ½-inch slices. Yield: 2 dozen.

CREAMY DARK FUDGE

3 (6-ounce) packages semisweet
   chocolate morsels
1 (14-ounce) can sweetened
   condensed milk
1½ teaspoons vanilla extract
⅓ cup chopped pecans

Combine chocolate morsels and condensed milk in a heavy saucepan. Cook over low heat until chocolate melts, stirring constantly. Remove from heat, and stir in vanilla.

Spread chocolate mixture in a lightly greased 8-inch square pan. Sprinkle with pecans. Chill 2 to 3 hours or until firm; cut into squares. Cover and store in refrigerator. Yield: 2 dozen.

TIGER BUTTER

1 pound white chocolate
1 (12-ounce) jar chunky peanut
   butter
1 pound semisweet chocolate,
   melted

Combine white chocolate and peanut butter in top of a double boiler; bring water to a boil. Reduce heat to low, and cook, stirring constantly, until chocolate melts. Spread mixture into a wax paper-lined 15- x 10- x 1-inch jellyroll pan.

Pour semisweet chocolate over peanut butter mixture, and swirl through with a knife. Chill until firm. Cut into 1½- x 1-inch pieces. Store in refrigerator. Yield: about 6 dozen.

AMARETTO DESSERT TRUFFLES

12 (1-ounce) squares semisweet
   chocolate
½ cup butter or margarine
2 egg yolks
½ cup whipping cream
¼ cup amaretto
   Finely chopped almonds
   or cocoa

Place chocolate in top of a double boiler; bring water to a boil. Reduce heat to low; cook until chocolate melts. Remove from heat; add butter 1 tablespoon at a time.

Beat egg yolks at medium speed of an electric mixer until thick and lemon colored. Gradually stir about one-fourth of hot mixture into yolks; add to remaining hot mixture, stirring constantly. Stir in whipping cream and amaretto.

Return to heat, and cook 1 minute or until mixture is thickened and smooth, stirring constantly.

Cover and chill at least 8 hours or until firm. Shape mixture into 1-inch balls; roll in chopped almonds or cocoa. Store in refrigerator. Yield: 3½ dozen.

ALMOND TRUFFLES

3 tablespoons butter, softened
½ cup sifted powdered sugar
6 (1-ounce) squares semisweet
   chocolate, finely grated
1 egg yolk, slightly beaten
2 tablespoons white
   crème de cacao
24 whole almonds, toasted
½ cup finely chopped almonds

Cream butter; gradually add sugar, beating well at medium speed of an electric mixer. Add chocolate, egg yolk, and crème de cacao; beat until blended. Cover and chill 1 hour.

Shape mixture into 1-inch balls, inserting one whole almond into center of each; roll in chopped almonds. Cover and chill at least 8 hours. Yield: about 2 dozen.

CHOCOLATE-RUM TRUFFLES

1 (6-ounce) package semisweet
    chocolate morsels
3 tablespoons unsalted butter
3 tablespoons powdered sugar
3 egg yolks
1 tablespoon rum
    Cocoa

Place chocolate morsels in top of a double boiler; bring water to a boil. Reduce heat to low; cook until chocolate melts. Add butter and powdered sugar, stirring until sugar dissolves. Remove from heat.

Add egg yolks, one at a time, beating at medium speed of an electric mixer. Stir in rum. Pour mixture into a bowl; cover, and let sit for 12 to 24 hours in a cool, dry place. (Do not refrigerate.)

Shape mixture into 1-inch balls; roll in cocoa. Freeze about 1 hour. Store in an airtight container in refrigerator. Yield: about 2 dozen.

CHOCOLATE DROPS

2 (16-ounce) packages powdered
    sugar, sifted
1½ cups sweetened condensed milk
½ cup butter or margarine, melted
1 teaspoon vanilla extract
2 cups chopped pecans
1 cup flaked coconut
1 (12-ounce) package semisweet
    chocolate morsels
3 tablespoons shortening

Combine sugar, sweetened condensed milk, butter, and vanilla; stir until smooth. Stir in pecans and coconut. Roll mixture into 1-inch balls, and chill at least 1 hour.

Combine chocolate and shortening in top of a double boiler; bring water to a boil. Reduce heat to low; cook until chocolate melts. Place several candy balls in chocolate mixture; roll with spoon to coat evenly. Remove from mixture with a wooden pick or spoon, allowing excess chocolate to drain. Place on wax paper to cool. Repeat procedure until all candy balls are coated. Cover and store in refrigerator. Yield: 9 dozen.

PROCESSOR CHOCOLATE VELVETS

12 ounces milk chocolate candy
¼ cup unsalted butter
¾ cup whipping cream, scalded
1½ tablespoons crème de cacao or
    Kahlúa
    Chocolate sprinkles or finely
    chopped pecans

Position knife blade in food processor bowl. Break chocolate into pieces, and place in bowl; process until finely chopped.

Heat butter to 110°. With processor running, add butter and hot whipping cream through feed chute; continue processing 1 minute. Stir in crème de cacao. Pour mixture into a bowl; cover and chill at least 8 hours.

Shape mixture into ¾-inch balls, and roll in chocolate sprinkles or chopped pecans. Freeze 1 hour or until firm. Store in refrigerator. Yield: 3 dozen.

CHOCOLATE BALLS

1 tablespoon cocoa
½ cup powdered sugar
¼ cup bourbon
1 tablespoon light corn syrup
½ cup finely ground pecans or
    walnuts
1¼ cups finely crushed vanilla wafers
2 egg whites, slightly beaten
12 ounces chocolate sprinkles

Sift cocoa and sugar together; set aside. Combine bourbon and corn syrup in a bowl; stir in cocoa mixture, pecans, and vanilla wafers.

Roll mixture into 1-inch balls; dip each in egg white, and roll in chocolate sprinkles. Store in a covered container. Yield: 1½ dozen.

CHOCOLATE MARBLES

2 cups (9½ ounces) amaretti
    almond cookie crumbs
¾ cup butter, softened
⅓ cup amaretto or other
    almond-flavored liqueur
1 (8-ounce) package semisweet
    chocolate morsels

Combine first 3 ingredients, stirring
well; chill. Shape into ¾-inch balls.

Place chocolate in top of a double boiler;
bring water to a boil. Reduce heat to low;
cook until chocolate melts. Dip each ball
into melted chocolate; chill 30 minutes or
until chocolate hardens. Store in an airtight container in refrigerator. Yield: about
5 dozen.

CHOCOLATE RUM BALLS

1 (6-ounce) package semisweet
    chocolate morsels
1 (7-ounce) jar marshmallow creme
1 tablespoon imitation rum extract
3 cups crisp rice cereal
½ cup shredded coconut
½ cup chopped pecans

Place chocolate in top of a double boiler;
bring water to a boil. Reduce heat to low;
cook until chocolate melts. Cool.

Combine melted chocolate, marshmallow creme, and rum extract; stir well. Add
cereal, coconut, and pecans, stirring
gently to blend. Shape into 1-inch balls.
Chill until firm. Yield: about 4½ dozen.

Note: Rum balls may be rolled in additional coconut or pecans, if desired.

OLD-FASHIONED MILLIONAIRES

1 (14-ounce) package caramels
3 to 4 tablespoons milk
2 cups pecan pieces
    Butter or margarine
1 tablespoon shortening
1 (12-ounce) package semisweet
    chocolate morsels

Melt caramels in milk over low heat; stir
in pecans. Drop by teaspoonfuls onto buttered wax paper. Chill. Melt shortening
and chocolate morsels in a heavy saucepan over low heat. Remove from heat; dip
candy into chocolate, and return to wax
paper. Chill. Yield: 3½ dozen.

MOCHA-BOURBON BALLS

12 (1-ounce) squares semisweet
    chocolate
½ cup butter
⅓ cup sugar
½ cup whipping cream
¼ cup bourbon
1 tablespoon instant coffee granules
2 cups ground pecans, divided
¾ cup chocolate wafer crumbs

Combine chocolate, butter, and sugar in
top of a double boiler; bring water to a boil.
Reduce heat to low; cook until chocolate
and butter melt. Remove from heat; stir in
cream, bourbon, coffee granules, and 1
cup pecans. Cover and chill until firm.

Combine remaining cup of pecans and
wafer crumbs; stir well. Shape chocolate
mixture into 1-inch balls and roll in crumb
mixture. Store in refrigerator. Yield: about
5 dozen.

CHOCOLATE-COVERED
RAISINS

1 (6-ounce) package semisweet
    chocolate morsels
¼ cup dark corn syrup
2 tablespoons powdered sugar
1½ teaspoons vanilla extract
2 cups raisins

Combine chocolate morsels and corn
syrup in top of a double boiler; bring water
to a boil. Reduce heat to low; cook until
chocolate melts, stirring constantly. Remove from heat, and stir in powdered
sugar, vanilla, and raisins. Drop by half-
teaspoonfuls onto wax paper; chill. Store
in refrigerator. Yield: about 5½ dozen.

PEANUT BUTTER CREAMS

¼ cup powdered sugar
½ cup sweetened condensed milk
1 cup creamy peanut butter
1 (6-ounce) package semisweet
    chocolate morsels
½ cup chocolate sprinkles

Combine sugar, condensed milk, and peanut butter in a medium mixing bowl; stir until well blended. Stir in chocolate morsels, and chill until firm. Shape into ¾-inch balls, and roll in chocolate sprinkles. Chill until firm. Yield: 6 to 7 dozen.

MIXED RAISIN CANDY

4 cups sugar
2 cups whipping cream
2 tablespoons light corn syrup
1 (9-ounce) package raisins
2 cups chopped pecans or walnuts
1 cup flaked coconut
2½ cups semisweet chocolate
    morsels
¼ cup plus 1½ teaspoons shortening

Combine first 3 ingredients in a heavy saucepan; stir well. Bring to a boil, stirring often, until mixture reaches soft ball stage (234°). Remove from heat; cover and chill 1 to 2 hours. Stir in raisins, pecans, and coconut; shape into 1-inch balls.

Combine chocolate and shortening in top of a double boiler; bring water to a boil. Reduce heat to low; cook until chocolate melts. Place several candy balls in chocolate mixture; coat evenly. Remove with a wooden pick or spoon, allowing excess chocolate to drain off. Place on wax paper to cool. Repeat procedure until all candy balls are coated. Cover and store in refrigerator. Yield: 8 dozen.

KENTUCKY COLONELS

½ cup butter, softened
3 tablespoons sweetened condensed
    milk
⅓ cup plus 2 teaspoons bourbon
7½ cups powdered sugar
½ cup finely chopped pecans
1 (6-ounce) package semisweet
    chocolate morsels
1 tablespoon shortening
    Pecan halves

Combine butter, condensed milk, and bourbon in a large mixing bowl; add sugar, and knead until mixture is blended and does not stick to hands. Knead in chopped pecans. Shape into 1-inch balls.

Combine chocolate morsels and shortening in top of a double boiler; bring water to a boil. Reduce heat to low; cook until chocolate melts.

Using a wooden pick, dip each ball of candy into chocolate mixture, allowing excess chocolate to drain off. Place on wax paper and gently press a pecan half on each. Yield: about 6 dozen.

CHOCOLATE BRITTLE

2 cups butter
2 cups sugar
¼ cup plus 2 tablespoons water
12 (1.05-ounce) milk chocolate
    candy bars
3 cups chopped pecans

Combine butter, sugar, and water in a Dutch oven; stir well. Cook over low heat, stirring occasionally, until candy reaches hard crack stage (300°). Lightly butter 2 12-inch pizza pans. Remove sugar mixture from heat and immediately pour into pans, spreading to edges of pans.

Place chocolate in top of a double boiler; bring water to a boil. Reduce heat to low, and cook until chocolate melts. Spread chocolate over brittle; sprinkle pecans evenly on top. Press pecans into chocolate. Cool until chocolate is firm. Break candy into pieces. Yield: about 4 pounds.

BUTTER-NUT CRUNCHIES

1 cup sugar
½ cup butter or margarine
¼ cup water
½ teaspoon salt
1½ cups walnuts, finely chopped and
   divided
1 (12-ounce) package semisweet
   chocolate morsels

Combine sugar, butter, water, and salt in a heavy saucepan; stir well. Bring to a boil; cook, stirring occasionally, until mixture reaches soft crack stage (285°). Stir in ½ cup walnuts. Pour into a buttered 15- x 10- x 1-inch jellyroll pan, spreading to about ¼-inch thickness. Cool.

Melt chocolate morsels in a heavy saucepan over low heat, stirring constantly; spread half of chocolate over cooled candy. Sprinkle with ½ cup walnuts; lightly press walnuts into chocolate. Cool until firm. Invert candy; repeat procedure with remaining chocolate and walnuts. Cool; break into pieces. Store in an airtight container. Yield: about 1 pound.

WHITE CHOCOLATE SALTIES

1 pound white chocolate
2 tablespoons shortening
3 cups pretzel sticks
1 cup salted Spanish peanuts

Combine chocolate and shortening in top of a double boiler; bring water to a boil. Reduce heat to low; cook until chocolate melts. Pour chocolate mixture into a large mixing bowl. Stir in pretzels and peanuts; spread into a buttered 15- x 10- x 1-inch jellyroll pan. Chill 20 minutes or until firm; break into pieces. Store in an airtight container. Yield: 1½ pounds.

CHOCOLATE-COVERED PRETZELS

1 (5.75-ounce) package milk
   chocolate morsels
2 tablespoons shortening
24 (3-inch) pretzels

Combine chocolate morsels and shortening in top of a double boiler; bring water to a boil. Reduce heat to low; cook until chocolate melts, stirring occasionally. Remove double boiler from heat, leaving chocolate mixture over hot water.

Dip each pretzel in chocolate; allow excess to drain. Place on wax paper-lined cookie sheets; chill until firm. Arrange pretzels between layers of wax paper in an airtight container; store in a cool place. Yield: 2 dozen.

ALMOND ROCA

2 cups butter
2 cups sugar
2 cups finely chopped almonds,
   toasted and divided
1 pound milk chocolate

Melt butter in a Dutch oven; add sugar, and cook over medium-high heat until mixture comes to a boil. Reduce heat to medium, and boil 5 minutes, stirring frequently. Add 1 cup almonds and cook, stirring constantly, until mixture reaches hard crack stage (300°). Remove from heat, and immediately pour onto two buttered aluminum foil-covered cookie sheets, spreading to about ¼-inch thickness. Cool until candy is hard.

Place chocolate in top of a double boiler; bring water to a boil. Reduce heat to low, and cook until chocolate melts. Working quickly, spread half of chocolate over cooled candy; sprinkle ½ cup almonds evenly on top. Lightly press almonds into chocolate. Chill until firm. Invert candy onto foil, and repeat procedure.

When firm, break candy into pieces. If stored in refrigerator, allow candy to stand at room temperature 5 minutes before serving. Yield: about 3¾ pounds.

Cookies

CHOCOLATE-PEANUT COOKIES

    1 cup butter or margarine, softened
1½ cups sugar
    2 eggs
    2 teaspoons vanilla extract
    2 cups all-purpose flour
⅔ cup cocoa
¾ teaspoon baking soda
½ teaspoon salt
    1 cup finely chopped peanuts

Cream butter; gradually add sugar, beating at low speed of an electric mixer until light and fluffy. Stir in eggs and vanilla.

Combine flour, cocoa, soda, and salt; add to creamed mixture, beating well. Stir in peanuts.

Drop dough by teaspoonfuls onto ungreased cookie sheets. Bake at 350° for 12 to 14 minutes. Remove to wire racks to cool completely. Yield: about 5½ dozen.

CHOCOLATE-NUT CHEWS

1½ cups sugar
½ cup cocoa
½ cup evaporated milk
⅓ cup butter or margarine
⅓ cup peanut butter
1½ cups quick-cooking oats, uncooked
½ cup chopped pecans or walnuts
    1 teaspoon vanilla extract

Combine sugar, cocoa, milk, and butter in a heavy saucepan. Cook over medium heat, stirring constantly, until mixture reaches a slow boil (mixture will bubble around sides). Cook 2 additional minutes, stirring constantly.

Remove from heat; add peanut butter, and stir until smooth. Stir in oats, pecans, and vanilla. Drop by tablespoonfuls onto wax paper; cool. Yield: about 4½ dozen.

CHOCOLATE CHIP COOKIES

½ cup butter or margarine, softened
½ cup sugar
¼ cup firmly packed dark brown
    sugar
1 egg
1 teaspoon vanilla extract
1½ cups all-purpose flour
½ teaspoon baking soda
¼ teaspoon salt
1 (6-ounce) package semisweet
    chocolate morsels
½ cup chopped pecans

Cream butter; gradually add sugar, beating at low speed of an electric mixer until light and fluffy. Add egg and vanilla; beat well. Combine flour, soda, and salt; add to creamed mixture, beating well. Stir in chocolate morsels and pecans.

Drop dough by heaping teaspoonfuls onto ungreased cookie sheets. Bake at 350° for 10 to 12 minutes. Cool slightly on cookie sheets; remove to wire racks to cool completely. Yield: 4 dozen.

CHOCOLATE DROP COOKIES

½ cup shortening
1 cup firmly packed brown sugar
1 egg, beaten
2 (1-ounce) squares semisweet
    chocolate, melted
1 teaspoon vanilla extract
1⅔ cups sifted cake flour
½ teaspoon baking soda
½ teaspoon salt
½ cup milk
½ cup chopped pecans or walnuts
    Chocolate-Coffee Frosting

Cream shortening; gradually sugar, beating at low speed of an electric mixer until light and fluffy. Add egg, chocolate, and vanilla; beat well.

Combine flour, soda, and salt; add to creamed mixture alternately with milk, stirring well. Stir in pecans.

Drop dough by teaspoonfuls, about 1½ inches apart, onto greased cookie sheets. Bake at 350° for 10 to 12 minutes or until

done. Remove to wire racks and frost with Chocolate-Coffee Frosting while still warm. Yield: about 4 dozen.

Chocolate-Coffee Frosting:

¼ cup plus 2 tablespoons cocoa
¼ cup plus 2 tablespoons hot coffee
¼ cup plus 2 tablespoons butter or
    margarine, melted
1 teaspoon vanilla extract
3 cups sifted powdered sugar

Combine first 4 ingredients; blend until smooth. Add powdered sugar, stirring well. Yield: enough for about 4 dozen.

CHOCOLATE CHIP-OATMEAL COOKIES

1 cup butter or margarine, softened
¾ cup sugar
¾ cup firmly packed brown sugar
2 eggs
1 teaspoon vanilla extract
1½ cups all-purpose flour
1 teaspoon baking soda
½ teaspoon baking powder
½ teaspoon salt
2 cups quick-cooking oats,
    uncooked
1 (12-ounce) package semisweet
    chocolate morsels
1 cup chopped pecans

Cream butter; gradually add sugar, beating at low speed of an electric mixer until light and fluffy. Add eggs and vanilla; beat well. Combine flour, soda, baking powder, and salt; add to creamed mixture, beating well. Stir in remaining ingredients.

Drop dough by heaping teaspoonfuls onto ungreased cookie sheets; bake at 375° for 8 to 10 minutes. Cool slightly on cookie sheets; remove to wire racks to cool completely. Yield: about 7½ dozen.

DELUXE CHOCOLATE CHIP COOKIES

1 cup butter or margarine, softened
2 cups firmly packed brown sugar
2 eggs
1 teaspoon vanilla extract
2 cups all-purpose flour
½ teaspoon baking powder
2 cups crisp rice cereal
1 (6-ounce) package semisweet
    chocolate morsels
1 cup shredded coconut
1 cup chopped pecans or walnuts

Cream butter; add sugar, beating at low speed of an electric mixer until light and fluffy. Add eggs and vanilla; beat well.

Combine flour and baking powder; add to creamed mixture. Add remaining ingredients, stirring well.

Drop dough by heaping teaspoonfuls onto lightly greased baking sheets. Bake at 350° for 10 to 12 minutes or until lightly browned. Remove to wire racks to cool completely. Yield: about 7½ dozen.

NATURE'S CHOCOLATE CHIP COOKIES

1 cup butter or margarine, softened
¾ cup firmly packed brown sugar
¾ cup sugar
2 eggs
1 teaspoon vanilla extract
1¼ cups all-purpose flour
1 cup whole wheat flour
½ teaspoon baking powder
1 teaspoon baking soda
¼ teaspoon salt
1 (12-ounce) package semisweet
    chocolate morsels
½ cup salted sunflower kernels
¼ cup sesame seeds

Cream butter; gradually add sugar, beating at low speed of an electric mixer until light and fluffy. Add eggs and vanilla; beat well. Combine flour, baking powder, soda, and salt; add to creamed mixture, beating well. Stir in remaining ingredients.

Drop dough by heaping teaspoonfuls onto lightly greased cookie sheets. Bake at 375° for 8 to 10 minutes. Cool slightly on cookie sheets; remove to wire racks to cool completely. Yield: 5 dozen.

GIANT CHOCOLATE CHIP COOKIES

1 cup butter or margarine, softened
1 cup firmly packed brown sugar
½ cup sugar
2 eggs
2¼ cups all-purpose flour
1 teaspoon baking soda
½ teaspoon salt
1 teaspoon vanilla extract
1½ cups semisweet chocolate
    morsels
¾ cup chopped pecans

Cream butter; gradually add sugar, beating at low speed of an electric mixer until light and fluffy. Add eggs, and beat until blended.

Combine flour, soda, and salt. Add to creamed mixture, stirring well. Stir in vanilla, chocolate morsels, and pecans.

Divide mixture into thirds. Spoon each third onto an ungreased cookie sheet, spreading into an 8½-inch circle. Bake at 375° for 12 to 14 minutes or until lightly browned. Gently remove cookies to wire racks to cool completely. Yield: three 10-inch cookies.

CHOCOLATE-MINT CHIP COOKIES

2 (1-ounce) squares unsweetened
    chocolate
½ cup butter or margarine, softened
1 cup sugar
2 eggs
½ teaspoon vanilla extract
2 cups all-purpose flour
1 teaspoon baking powder
⅛ teaspoon salt
6 ounces mint chips, cut into small
    pieces

Place chocolate in top of a double boiler; bring water to a boil. Reduce heat to low; cook until chocolate melts. Set aside to cool slightly.

Cream butter; gradually add sugar, beating at medium speed of an electric mixer. Add eggs, one at a time, beating well after each addition. Stir in vanilla.

Combine flour, baking powder, and salt; add to creamed mixture, beating well. Stir in chocolate; mix well. Stir in mint chips.

Drop dough by rounded teaspoonfuls onto lightly greased cookie sheets. Bake at 350° for 8 to 10 minutes. Cool slightly on cookie sheets; remove to wire racks to cool completely. Yield: 5 dozen.

ORANGE-CHOCOLATE COOKIES

½ cup shortening
1 (3-ounce) package cream cheese, softened
½ cup sugar
1 egg, beaten
1 teaspoon vanilla extract
1 teaspoon grated orange rind
1 cup all-purpose flour
½ teaspoon salt
1 (6-ounce) package semisweet chocolate morsels

Combine first 4 ingredients in a large bowl; beat at low speed of an electric mixer until smooth and creamy. Add vanilla and orange rind; beat well. Combine flour and salt; add to creamed mixture, beating well. Stir in chocolate morsels.

Drop dough by heaping teaspoonfuls onto ungreased cookie sheets; bake at 350° for 15 minutes or until edges just begin to brown. Remove to wire racks to cool completely. Yield: 3 dozen.

CHOCOLATE CRISPY COOKIES

½ cup butter or margarine, softened
1 cup sugar
1 egg
1 teaspoon vanilla extract
1¼ cups all-purpose flour
½ teaspoon baking soda
¼ teaspoon salt
2 cups crisp rice cereal
1 (6-ounce) package semisweet chocolate morsels

Cream butter; gradually add sugar, beating at low speed of an electric mixer until light and fluffy. Add egg and vanilla; beat well. Combine flour, soda, and salt; add to creamed mixture, beating well. Stir in rice cereal and chocolate morsels.

Drop dough by heaping teaspoonfuls onto lightly greased cookie sheets. Bake at 350° for 13 minutes. Cool slightly on cookie sheets; remove to wire racks to cool completely. Yield: 3½ dozen.

NUGGET COOKIES

1 cup butter, softened
¾ cup sugar
¾ cup firmly packed brown sugar
2 eggs
2½ cups all-purpose flour
1 teaspoon baking soda
1 teaspoon salt
2 teaspoons vanilla extract
1 (6-ounce) package semisweet chocolate morsels
1 cup chopped pecans
2 cups seedless raisins

Cream butter; gradually add sugar, beating at low speed of an electric mixer until light and fluffy. Add eggs, one at a time, beating well after each addition. Combine flour, soda, and salt; add to creamed mixture, beating 1 minute. Stir in vanilla, chocolate morsels, pecans, and raisins.

Drop dough by teaspoonfuls onto lightly greased cookie sheets. Bake at 375° for 10 to 12 minutes or until golden brown. Remove to wire racks to cool completely. Yield: about 2½ dozen.

CHOCOLATE MACAROONS

1 (18.5-ounce) package devil's food
  cake mix with pudding
1 cup flaked coconut, toasted
½ cup regular oats, uncooked and
  toasted
¾ cup butter or margarine, melted
2 teaspoons vanilla extract
2 eggs, slightly beaten
6 (1.45-ounce) milk chocolate
  candy bars, broken into squares
¾ cup flaked coconut

Combine first 6 ingredients; chill 30
minutes. Drop dough by heaping teaspoonfuls 2 inches apart on ungreased
cookie sheets. Bake at 350° for 10 minutes. Immediately top each cookie with
one chocolate square; spread to frost.
Sprinkle cookies with coconut. Yield:
about 6 dozen.

FORGET 'EM COOKIES

2 egg whites
  Dash of salt
¾ cup sugar
1 teaspoon vanilla extract
1 (6-ounce) package semisweet
  chocolate morsels
1 cup chopped pecans

Preheat oven to 350°. Beat egg whites
(at room temperature) at high speed of an
electric mixer until foamy; add salt. Gradually add sugar, 1 tablespoon at a time,
beating until stiff peaks form.
Fold vanilla, chocolate morsels, and
pecans into beaten egg whites. Drop by
teaspoonfuls onto aluminum foil-lined
cookie sheets. Place in oven, and immediately turn off heat. Do not open oven door
for at least 8 hours. Carefully remove from
aluminum foil. Yield: about 3 dozen.

CHEWY CHOCOLATE COOKIES

1½ cups butter or margarine,
  softened
1 cup sugar
1 cup firmly packed brown sugar
3 eggs
2 teaspoons vanilla extract
4½ cups all-purpose flour
2 teaspoons baking soda
½ teaspoon salt
1 cup chopped pecans
1 (6-ounce) package semisweet
  chocolate morsels

Cream butter; gradually add sugar, beating at low speed of an electric mixer until
light and fluffy. Add eggs and vanilla, beating well.
Combine flour, soda, and salt; add to
creamed mixture, beating just until
blended. Stir in chopped pecans and chocolate morsels.
Shape dough into 3 long rolls, 2 inches
in diameter. Wrap each roll in wax paper,
and freeze at least 8 hours.
Unwrap rolls, and cut into ¼-inch
slices; place on ungreased cookie sheets.
Bake at 350° for 12 to 14 minutes or until
lightly browned. Remove to wire racks to
cool completely. Yield: about 7 dozen.

JUMBO CHOCOLATE SNAPPERS

1 (6-ounce) package semisweet
  chocolate morsels
⅔ cup shortening
½ cup sugar
1 egg
¼ cup corn syrup
1¾ cups all-purpose flour
2 teaspoons baking soda
¼ teaspoon salt
1 teaspoon ground cinnamon
  Sugar

Place chocolate morsels in top of a double boiler; bring water to a boil. Reduce
heat to low; cook until chocolate melts.
Remove from heat.
Cream shortening; gradually add ½ cup
sugar, beating at low speed of an electric

mixer until light and fluffy. Add chocolate, egg, and corn syrup, beating well.

Combine flour, soda, salt, and cinnamon; add to creamed mixture, beating just until blended.

Shape dough into balls, using about 3 tablespoons dough for each ball, and roll in sugar. Place on ungreased cookie sheets about 2½ inches apart; bake at 350° for 18 minutes. Cool on cookie sheets 2 minutes. Remove to wire racks to cool completely. Yield: about 14 jumbo cookies.

Note: For smaller cookies, use 1 tablespoon dough. Bake at 350° for 15 minutes. Yield: about 3½ dozen.

CHOCOLATE SNOWBALL COOKIES

¼ **cup butter or margarine, softened**
½ **cup sugar**
1 **egg**
1 **(1-ounce) square unsweetened chocolate, melted**
1 **teaspoon vanilla extract**
1½ **cups all-purpose flour**
½ **teaspoon baking powder**
¼ **teaspoon salt**
   Snowy Glaze

Cream butter; gradually add sugar, beating at low speed of an electric mixer until light and fluffy. Add next 3 ingredients, beating well.

Combine flour, baking powder, and salt; gradually add to creamed mixture, beating just until smooth. Chill 1 to 2 hours.

Shape dough into 1-inch balls. Place on greased cookie sheets, and bake at 350° for 12 minutes. Remove to wire racks to cool completely. Dip tops of cookies in Snowy Glaze. Store in an airtight container. Yield: about 3 dozen.

Snowy Glaze:

1 **cup sifted powdered sugar**
1 **tablespoon plus 2 teaspoons milk**
½ **teaspoon vanilla extract**

Combine all ingredients; beat until smooth. Yield: enough for about 3 dozen.

COCOA KISS COOKIES

1 **cup butter or margarine, softened**
⅔ **cup sugar**
1 **teaspoon vanilla extract**
1⅔ **cups all-purpose flour**
¼ **cup cocoa**
1 **cup coarsely ground walnuts**
1 **(9-ounce) package milk chocolate kisses, unwrapped**

Cream butter; gradually add sugar, beating at low speed of an electric mixer until light and fluffy. Add vanilla, stirring well. Add flour and cocoa, stirring well. Stir in walnuts. Chill dough 2 hours or until firm.

Wrap 1 tablespoon of dough around each chocolate kiss, and roll to form a ball. Place on ungreased cookie sheets; bake at 375° for 12 minutes. Cool slightly on cookie sheets; remove to wire racks to cool completely. Yield: about 4 dozen.

CHOCOLATE CHIP MELT-AWAYS

1 **cup butter or margarine, softened**
1 **cup vegetable oil**
1 **cup sugar**
1 **cup sifted powdered sugar**
2 **eggs**
4 **cups all-purpose flour**
1 **teaspoon baking soda**
1 **teaspoon cream of tartar**
1 **teaspoon salt**
1 **teaspoon vanilla extract**
1 **(12-ounce) package semisweet chocolate morsels**
   Additional sugar

Combine first 5 ingredients in a large mixing bowl; beat at low speed of an electric mixer until smooth. Combine flour, soda, cream of tartar, and salt; add to butter mixture, beating until smooth. Stir in vanilla and chocolate morsels.

Shape dough into 1-inch balls; roll in sugar. Place balls 2 inches apart on ungreased cookie sheets; bake at 375° for 10 to 12 minutes or until lightly browned. Remove to wire racks to cool completely. Yield: about 8½ dozen.

CHOCOLATE-CHERRY COOKIES

1 cup butter or margarine, softened
1 cup sifted powdered sugar
1 egg
¼ teaspoon almond extract
2 (1-ounce) squares semisweet
    chocolate, melted and cooled
2½ cups all-purpose flour
¼ teaspoon cream of tartar
1 cup red candied cherries, coarsely
    chopped
½ cup finely chopped pecans

Cream butter; gradually add sugar, beating at low speed of an electric mixer until light and fluffy. Add egg, beating well; stir in almond extract. Stir in melted chocolate, mixing well. Combine flour and cream of tartar; add to creamed mixture, stirring well. Stir in cherries and pecans.

Shape dough into two 10- x 2-inch blocks or rolls. Wrap in plastic wrap; freeze several hours or overnight.

Cut dough into ¼-inch slices; place on ungreased cookie sheets. Bake at 375° for 10 to 12 minutes. Remove to wire racks to cool completely. Yield: 5 dozen.

CHOCOLATE PINWHEEL COOKIES

1 (1-ounce) square unsweetened
    chocolate
½ cup butter or margarine, softened
¾ cup sugar
1 egg
1 teaspoon vanilla extract
1¼ cups all-purpose flour
¼ teaspoon baking powder
¼ teaspoon salt

Place chocolate in top of a double boiler; bring water to a boil. Reduce heat to low; cook until chocolate melts. Set aside to cool slightly.

Cream butter; gradually add sugar, beating at medium speed of an electric mixer until light and fluffy. Add egg and vanilla, beating well. Combine flour, baking powder, and salt; gradually add to creamed mixture, stirring well. Halve dough; stir

melted chocolate into one portion. Cover and chill dough 2 hours.

Roll each portion of dough out to a 12- x 10-inch rectangle on lightly floured plastic wrap. (Dough will be soft.) Invert chocolate dough onto plain dough; peel off plastic wrap. Press chocolate dough firmly with a rolling pin; roll up jellyroll fashion starting with long side. Cover and chill at least 8 hours.

Cut dough with an electric knife into ¼-inch-thick slices; place on lightly greased cookie sheets. Bake at 350° for 12 to 14 minutes. Remove to wire racks to cool completely. Yield: about 4 dozen.

BROWNIE WAFFLE COOKIES

⅓ cup shortening
1 (1-ounce) square unsweetened
    chocolate
1 egg, beaten
½ cup sugar
2 tablespoons milk
½ teaspoon vanilla extract
¾ cup all-purpose flour
½ teaspoon baking powder
¼ teaspoon salt
1 cup finely chopped pecans,
    divided

Combine shortening and chocolate in a heavy saucepan. Place over low heat, stirring constantly, until melted; cool. Combine egg, sugar, milk, and vanilla in a bowl. Stir in chocolate mixture.

Combine flour, baking powder, and salt; add to chocolate mixture. Add ⅔ cup pecans, stirring well.

Preheat waffle iron at medium heat. Drop batter by level tablespoonfuls onto iron, about 2 inches apart. Sprinkle with remaining ⅓ cup pecans. Close iron, and bake about 3 minutes or until done. Remove to wire racks to cool completely. Yield: 2 dozen.

CHOCOLATE-MINT SNAPS

4 (1-ounce) squares unsweetened
    chocolate
1¼ cups shortening
2 cups sugar
2 eggs
⅓ cup corn syrup
2½ tablespoons water
2 teaspoons peppermint extract
1 teaspoon vanilla extract
4 cups all-purpose flour
2 teaspoons baking soda
½ teaspoon salt
¼ cup plus 2 tablespoons sugar

Place chocolate in top of a double boiler; bring water to a boil. Reduce heat to low; cook until chocolate melts.

Cream shortening; gradually add 2 cups sugar, beating at low speed of an electric mixer until light and fluffy. Add melted chocolate, eggs, corn syrup, water, and flavorings; mix well. Combine flour, soda, and salt; add to creamed mixture, beating just until blended.

Shape dough into 1-inch balls, and roll in ¼ cup plus 2 tablespoons sugar. Place on ungreased cookie sheets; bake at 350° for 10 minutes. Cool on cookie sheets 5 minutes; remove to wire racks to cool completely. Yield: 10½ dozen.

CHOCOLATE CHIP BROWNIES

¼ cup butter or margarine, softened
¾ cup sugar
¼ cup light corn syrup
2 eggs, beaten
1 teaspoon vanilla extract
2 (1-ounce) squares unsweetened
    chocolate, melted
1 cup all-purpose flour
½ teaspoon baking powder
½ teaspoon salt
½ cup semisweet chocolate morsels
½ cup chopped walnuts

Cream butter; gradually add sugar, beating well at low speed of an electric mixer. Add corn syrup, eggs, and vanilla; beat well. Stir in melted chocolate.

Combine flour, baking powder, and salt; stir into creamed mixture. Stir in chocolate morsels and walnuts.

Spread mixture into a lightly greased 9-inch square baking pan. Bake at 350° for 25 to 30 minutes. Cool and cut into 1½-inch squares. Yield: 3 dozen.

AMARETTO BROWNIES

1 cup shortening
4 (1-ounce) squares unsweetened
    chocolate
2 cups sugar
4 eggs, beaten
2 tablespoons amaretto or other
    almond-flavored liqueur
1½ cups all-purpose flour
½ teaspoon salt
    Amaretto Frosting
3 to 4 tablespoons sliced almonds

Combine shortening and chocolate in a heavy saucepan; cook over low heat, stirring constantly, until melted. Add sugar, stirring well. Remove from heat, and cool. Stir in eggs and amaretto.

Combine flour and salt; add to creamed mixture, stirring well. Pour batter into a lightly greased 13- x 9- x 2-inch baking pan. Bake at 400° for 20 minutes; cool. Frost with Amaretto Frosting. Arrange almonds over top, and cut into 2-inch squares. Yield: about 2 dozen.

Amaretto Frosting:

¼ cup butter or margarine
1 (1-ounce) square unsweetened
    chocolate
2 tablespoons half-and-half
2½ cups sifted powdered sugar
    Dash of salt
2 tablespoons amaretto or other
    almond-flavored liqueur

Combine butter and chocolate in a heavy saucepan; cook over low heat, stirring constantly, until melted. Stir in half-and-half. Add powdered sugar, salt, and amaretto, stirring until thick enough to spread. Yield: enough for about 2 dozen.

CHOCOLATE-PECAN BROWNIES

2 (1-ounce) squares unsweetened
   chocolate
½ cup butter or margarine
1 cup sugar
½ cup all-purpose flour
1 teaspoon baking powder
2 eggs
1 teaspoon vanilla extract
1 cup chopped pecans

Combine chocolate and butter in top of a double boiler; bring water to a boil. Reduce heat to low, and cook, stirring constantly, until chocolate melts.

Combine sugar, flour, and baking powder in a mixing bowl; add chocolate mixture, mixing well. Add eggs; mix well. Stir in vanilla and pecans. Pour mixture into a greased 9-inch square baking pan. Bake at 350° for 25 to 30 minutes. Cool and cut into 1½-inch squares. Yield: 3 dozen.

FROSTED COCOA BROWNIES

2 cups sugar
2 cups self-rising flour
1 teaspoon baking soda
¼ cup plus 1 tablespoon cocoa
1 cup butter or margarine
1 cup water
½ cup buttermilk
2 eggs, beaten
1 teaspoon vanilla extract
   Frosting (recipe follows)

Combine sugar, flour, soda, and cocoa; stir well, and set aside.

Combine butter and water in a small saucepan; cook over medium heat, stirring occasionally, until butter melts. Pour over flour mixture. Beat at medium speed of an electric mixer about 1 minute. Add buttermilk, eggs, and vanilla; beat just until blended.

Pour into a greased and floured 18- x 12- x 1-inch jellyroll pan. Bake at 400° for 15 to 20 minutes or until a wooden pick inserted in center comes out clean.

Spread frosting over brownies. Cool and cut into 2-inch squares. Yield: 4½ dozen.

Frosting:

1 (16-ounce) package powdered
   sugar, sifted
   Dash of salt
¼ cup cocoa
½ cup butter or margarine
⅓ cup milk
1 teaspoon vanilla extract
1 cup chopped pecans

Combine sugar, salt, and cocoa; stir well, and set aside.

Combine butter and milk in a heavy saucepan. Cook over low heat, stirring occasionally, until butter melts. Pour into cocoa mixture; beat until thick enough to spread. Stir in vanilla and pecans. Yield: enough for 4½ dozen.

CRÈME DE MENTHE BROWNIES

½ cup butter or margarine, softened
1 cup sugar
4 eggs
1 cup all-purpose flour
½ teaspoon salt
1 (16-ounce) can chocolate syrup
1 teaspoon vanilla extract
¼ cup butter or margarine, softened
2 cups sifted powdered sugar
2 tablespoons crème de menthe
1 (6-ounce) package semisweet
   chocolate morsels
¼ cup butter or margarine

Cream ½ cup butter; gradually add 1 cup sugar, beating at low speed of an electric mixer until light and fluffy. Add eggs, one at a time, beating well after each addition.

Combine flour and salt; add to creamed mixture alternately with chocolate syrup, beginning and ending with flour mixture. Stir in vanilla.

Pour batter into a greased and floured 13- x 9- x 2-inch baking pan. Bake at 350° for 25 to 28 minutes. Cool completely. (Brownies will shrink from sides of pan while cooling.)

Cream ¼ cup butter; gradually add 2 cups powdered sugar and crème de menthe, mixing well. Spread evenly over brownies; chill 1 hour.

Combine chocolate morsels and remaining ¼ cup butter in top of a double boiler; bring water to a boil. Reduce heat to low; cook until chocolate melts. Spread over brownies; chill 1 hour. Cut into 2- x 1½-inch bars. Yield: about 3 dozen.

CHOCOLATE DREAM SQUARES

½ cup butter or margarine
¼ cup plus 1 tablespoon cocoa
¼ cup sugar
1 egg, slightly beaten
1 teaspoon vanilla extract
1 cup flaked coconut
½ cup chopped pecans
2 cups graham cracker crumbs
  Custard filling (recipe follows)
1 (6-ounce) package semisweet
  chocolate morsels
1 tablespoon butter or margarine

Combine first 4 ingredients in top of a double boiler; bring water to a boil. Reduce heat to low; cook until mixture thickens, stirring constantly. Remove from heat. Add vanilla, coconut, pecans, and cracker crumbs; mix well. Press mixture into a 9-inch square pan; chill 15 minutes.

Spread custard filling over chocolate. Chill 30 minutes or until custard mixture becomes firm.

Combine chocolate morsels and butter in a small saucepan; cook over low heat, stirring until chocolate melts. Spread over custard filling. Cool and cut into 1½-inch squares. Cover and store in refrigerator. Yield: 3 dozen.

Custard Filling:

¼ cup butter or margarine, softened
3 tablespoons milk
2 tablespoons vanilla instant
  pudding mix
2 cups sifted powdered sugar

Cream butter; add milk and pudding mix, beating until well blended. Add powdered sugar, and mix well. Yield: 1 cup.

BLACK WALNUT BROWNIES

½ cup butter or margarine, softened
1 cup sugar
2 eggs, beaten
1 teaspoon vanilla extract
¼ teaspoon salt
⅔ cup all-purpose flour
2 (1-ounce) squares unsweetened
  chocolate, melted
⅔ cup black walnuts, chopped

Cream butter; gradually add sugar, beating at low speed of an electric mixer until light and fluffy. Add eggs, vanilla, salt, and flour; mix well. Stir in chocolate and nuts. Pour into a greased 8-inch square baking pan. Bake at 325° for 20 minutes or until done. Cut into 2-inch squares. Yield: about 1½ dozen.

CHOCOLATE CHIP-TOFFEE GRAHAMS

11 whole graham crackers (4½- x
  2¼-inches), broken into
  squares
1 cup butter or margarine
1 cup sugar
1 teaspoon ground cinnamon
½ cup finely chopped pecans
1 (6-ounce) package semisweet
  chocolate mini-morsels

Arrange graham cracker squares in a single layer in a 15- x 10- x 1-inch jellyroll pan. Combine butter and sugar in a saucepan. Bring to a boil over medium heat, stirring constantly until butter melts; boil 2 minutes. Remove from heat, and stir in cinnamon and pecans. Pour mixture evenly over crackers; spread to edges of pan, covering crackers completely. Bake at 350° for 10 to 12 minutes.

Remove from oven, and sprinkle with chocolate morsels. Cool in pan 5 minutes; carefully separate and transfer cookies to wax paper-lined cookie sheets using a spatula. Refrigerate until chocolate hardens. Store cookies, layered between pieces of wax paper, in airtight containers in refrigerator. Yield: about 2 dozen.

BUTTERSCOTCH-MARSHMALLOW BROWNIES

½ cup butterscotch morsels
¼ cup butter or margarine
¾ cup all-purpose flour
⅓ cup firmly packed brown sugar
1 teaspoon baking powder
¼ teaspoon salt
1 egg, slightly beaten
½ teaspoon vanilla extract
1 cup semisweet chocolate morsels
1 cup miniature marshmallows
½ cup chopped pecans

Combine butterscotch morsels and butter in a small saucepan. Cook over medium heat, stirring occasionally, until morsels melt; set aside.

Combine next 4 ingredients; add butterscotch mixture, egg, and vanilla, mixing well. Stir in chocolate morsels, marshmallows, and pecans. Spread mixture in a greased 9-inch square baking pan. Bake at 350° for 20 to 25 minutes. (Brownies will have a chewy texture.) Cool and cut into 1½-inch squares. Yield: 3 dozen.

CHOCOLATE TEA BROWNIES

5 (1-ounce) squares unsweetened chocolate
⅔ cup butter or margarine
5 eggs
2½ cups sugar
2 teaspoons vanilla extract
½ teaspoon salt
1¼ cups all-purpose flour
1½ cups chopped pecans
    Chocolate frosting (recipe follows)
    Pecan halves

Combine chocolate and butter in a medium saucepan. Cook over low heat until chocolate melts.

Combine eggs, sugar, vanilla, and salt; beat at medium speed of an electric mixer until blended. Stir in flour, chopped pecans, and chocolate mixture.

Pour batter into a lightly greased 15- x 10- x 1-inch jellyroll pan. Bake at 350° for 25 minutes or until a wooden pick inserted in center comes out clean. Spread with chocolate frosting while brownies are still warm. Cut into 2-inch squares; top each with a pecan half. Yield: about 3 dozen.

Chocolate Frosting:

¼ cup plus 2 tablespoons butter or margarine
1½ (1-ounce) squares unsweetened chocolate, melted
3 tablespoons half-and-half
3 cups sifted powdered sugar
2 tablespoons kirsch or other cherry-flavored liqueur

Combine first 3 ingredients in a medium saucepan; cook until butter and chocolate melt. Remove from heat, and stir in sugar and kirsch; beat until thick enough to spread. Yield: enough for about 3 dozen.

ALMOND-CHOCOLATE BARS

1 (8-ounce) package cream cheese, softened
¾ cup butter or margarine, softened
¾ cup sugar
2 cups all-purpose flour
½ teaspoon baking powder
1 teaspoon vanilla extract
1 (6-ounce) package semisweet chocolate morsels
½ cup sliced almonds, toasted

Combine cream cheese and butter in a mixing bowl; beat well at low speed of an electric mixer. Gradually add sugar, beating until light and fluffy. Combine flour and baking powder; add to creamed mixture, beating well. Stir in vanilla. Spread mixture evenly in an ungreased 13- x 9- x 2-inch baking pan. Bake at 375° for 15 minutes.

Sprinkle chocolate morsels immediately over baked layer; let stand 5 minutes or until chocolate melts. Spread chocolate evenly, to edge of pan. Sprinkle with almonds. Cool and cut into 3- x 1-inch bars. Yield: 3 dozen.

CHOCOLATE CHIP-PEANUT BUTTER BROWNIES

⅓ cup butter or margarine, softened
½ cup peanut butter
½ cup sugar
½ cup firmly packed brown sugar
2 eggs
1 cup all-purpose flour
1 teaspoon baking powder
¼ teaspoon salt
1 teaspoon vanilla extract
1 (6-ounce) package chocolate
 morsels

Cream butter and peanut butter. Gradually add sugar, beating at low speed of an electric mixer until light and fluffy. Add eggs, one at a time, beating well after each addition.

Combine flour, baking powder, and salt; add to creamed mixture, stirring well. Stir in vanilla and chocolate morsels.

Pour batter into a greased 8-inch square baking pan. Bake at 350° for 30 to 35 minutes. Cool and cut into 2-inch squares. Yield: about 1½ dozen.

HEAVENLY HASH BROWNIES

2 (1-ounce) squares unsweetened
 chocolate
½ cup butter or margarine
2 eggs
1 cup sugar
½ cup all-purpose flour
 Chocolate-Marshmallow Frosting

Combine chocolate and butter in top of a double boiler; bring water to a boil. Reduce heat to low; cook, stirring constantly, until chocolate melts. Cool.

Combine eggs and sugar; beat at medium speed of an electric mixer just until blended. Add chocolate mixture and flour; beat just until smooth. Pour into a greased 9-inch square baking pan. Bake at 350° for 25 to 30 minutes. Cool completely. Spread with Chocolate-Marshmallow Frosting. Cool and cut into 1½-inch squares. Yield: 3 dozen.

Chocolate-Marshmallow Frosting:

2 (1-ounce) squares unsweetened
 chocolate
½ cup butter or margarine
1½ cups sifted powdered sugar
1 egg
1 teaspoon vanilla extract
2 cups miniature marshmallows
1 cup chopped pecans or walnuts

Combine chocolate and butter in top of a double boiler; bring water to a boil. Reduce heat to low; cook, stirring constantly, until chocolate melts. Cool.

Combine powdered sugar, egg, vanilla, and chocolate mixture in a medium bowl; beat at medium speed of an electric mixer until smooth. Stir in marshmallows and pecans. Yield: enough for 3 dozen.

CHOCOLATE CHIP SCOTCH BARS

⅓ cup shortening
⅓ cup butter or margarine, softened
½ cup sugar
½ cup firmly packed brown sugar
1 egg
1 teaspoon vanilla extract
1½ cups all-purpose flour
½ teaspoon salt
1 (6-ounce) package semisweet
 chocolate morsels
1 (6-ounce) package butterscotch
 morsels
½ cup chopped pecans

Cream shortening and butter; gradually add sugar, beating at low speed of an electric mixer until light and fluffy. Beat in egg and vanilla. Add remaining ingredients, and mix well. Pour into an ungreased 13- x 9- x 2-inch baking pan. Bake at 375° for 20 to 25 minutes. Cut into 2- x 1-inch bars. Yield: 4½ dozen.

CHOCOLATE-CINNAMON SQUARES

2 cups all-purpose flour
1 teaspoon baking powder
1 cup sugar
1 tablespoon ground cinnamon
½ cup butter or margarine, softened
½ cup shortening
1 egg, slightly beaten
1 egg, separated
⅓ cup sugar
1 teaspoon ground cinnamon
1 (6-ounce) package semisweet chocolate morsels
½ cup chopped pecans

Combine first 4 ingredients in a large bowl. Add butter, shortening, egg, and egg yolk, mixing well. Press evenly into a lightly greased 15- x 10- x 1-inch jellyroll pan. Beat egg white slightly, and brush over mixture.

Combine ⅓ cup sugar, 1 teaspoon cinnamon, chocolate morsels, and pecans; sprinkle over bottom layer. Bake at 350° for 25 minutes. Cool and cut into 2-inch squares. Yield: about 3 dozen.

MERINGUE-CHOCOLATE CHIP BARS

1½ cups all-purpose flour
½ cup firmly packed brown sugar
½ cup butter or margarine, melted
1 (6-ounce) package semisweet chocolate morsels
1½ cups chopped pecans
3 egg whites
1 cup firmly packed brown sugar

Combine flour and ½ cup brown sugar in a small bowl. Stir in butter, blending well. Press mixture into an ungreased 13- x 9- x 2-inch baking pan. Sprinkle with chocolate morsels and pecans.

Beat egg whites (at room temperature) at high speed of an electric mixer until foamy. Gradually add 1 cup brown sugar, beating until stiff peaks form. Spread meringue over chocolate and pecans. Bake at 375° for 18 to 20 minutes. Cool and cut into 3- x 1-inch bars. Yield: 3 dozen.

BY-CRACKY BARS

¾ cup shortening
1 cup sugar
2 eggs
1¾ cups all-purpose flour
1 teaspoon salt
¼ teaspoon baking soda
⅓ cup milk
1 teaspoon vanilla extract
1 (1-ounce) square unsweetened chocolate, melted
¾ cup chopped walnuts
8 to 9 double graham crackers
1 (6-ounce) package semisweet chocolate morsels

Cream shortening and sugar. Add eggs, one at a time, beating well at low speed of an electric mixer.

Combine flour, salt, and soda; add to creamed mixture alternately with milk, mixing well after each addition. Add vanilla, stirring well.

Place one-third of batter in another bowl, and add unsweetened chocolate and walnuts to this mixture. Spread chocolate mixture in a greased 13- x 9- x 2-inch baking pan. Arrange 8 to 9 double graham crackers over batter.

Add chocolate morsels to remaining two-thirds batter, and drop by spoonfuls over crackers, spreading to cover. Bake at 375° for 25 minutes. Cool and cut into 3- x 1-inch bars. Yield: 3 dozen.

CHOCOLATE CHIP SQUARES

¾ cup butter or margarine, softened
1 cup firmly packed brown sugar
2 cups all-purpose flour
1 teaspoon vanilla extract
1 (6-ounce) package chocolate morsels
¾ cup chopped pecans

Cream butter; gradually add sugar, beating well. Stir in flour and vanilla.

Press into an ungreased 13- x 9- x 2-inch baking pan. Sprinkle with chocolate morsels and pecans. Bake at 350° for 15 to 20 minutes. Cool; cut into 1½-inch squares. Yield: about 4 dozen.

COCONUT-CHOCOLATE CHEWS

1½ cups graham cracker crumbs
½ cup butter or margarine, melted
1 (6-ounce) package semisweet
    chocolate morsels
1 (6-ounce) package butterscotch
    morsels
1¼ cups flaked coconut
1 cup chopped pecans
1 (14-ounce) can sweetened
    condensed milk

Combine crumbs and butter; stir well, and press into a 9-inch square baking pan. Layer chocolate morsels, butterscotch morsels, coconut, and pecans over crumb mixture. Pour milk evenly over top. Bake at 350° for 35 to 40 minutes. Cool and cut into 1½-inch squares. Yield: 3 dozen.

CHOCOLATE-PEPPERMINT SQUARES

½ cup butter or margarine, softened
1 cup sugar
2 eggs
½ cup all-purpose flour
    Pinch of salt
2 (1-ounce) squares unsweetened
    chocolate, melted
½ cup chopped pecans or walnuts
    Peppermint Filling
    Chocolate Glaze

Cream butter; gradually add sugar, beating at low speed of an electric mixer until light and fluffy. Add eggs, one at a time, beating well after each addition.

Combine flour and salt; add to creamed mixture, beating well. Add chocolate, beating until blended; stir in pecans.

Pour batter into a greased 9-inch square baking pan. Bake at 350° for 20 minutes. Cool (layer will fall while cooling).

Spread Peppermint Filling over layer, and chill (filling will be very thin).

Drizzle chocolate glaze over filling; chill thoroughly. Cut into 1-inch squares. Store in refrigerator. Yield: about 7 dozen.

Peppermint Filling:

1 cup sifted powdered sugar
2 tablespoons butter or margarine,
    softened
1 tablespoon milk
½ to ¾ teaspoon peppermint extract

Combine all ingredients, beating until smooth. Yield: about ½ cup.

Chocolate Glaze:

2 (1-ounce) squares semisweet
    chocolate, melted
1 tablespoon butter or margarine,
    melted

Combine ingredients; stir well. Yield: about ¼ cup.

Desserts

HOT FUDGE PUDDING

- 1 cup self-rising flour
- 1¾ cups sugar, divided
- ¼ cup cocoa, divided
- ½ cup milk
- 2 tablespoons butter, melted
- 1 teaspoon vanilla extract
  Pinch of salt
- 1½ cups hot water
  Whipped cream or ice cream
  (optional)

Combine flour, ¾ cup sugar, and 2 tablespoons cocoa; stir in milk, butter, and vanilla. Pour mixture into a 9-inch square baking pan.

Combine remaining cup of sugar, remaining 2 tablespoons cocoa, and salt; sprinkle over flour mixture. Pour water over top; bake at 350° for 30 minutes. Serve warm with whipped cream or ice cream, if desired. Yield: 6 servings.

CHOCOLATE BREAD PUDDING

- 3 cups soft breadcrumbs
- ¼ cup cocoa
- ½ cup chopped pecans or walnuts
- 2 eggs
- ½ cup sugar
- 3 cups milk
- 1 teaspoon vanilla extract
- ¼ teaspoon salt
  Whipped cream (optional)

Combine breadcrumbs, cocoa, and pecans, stirring well; set aside.

Beat eggs with a wire whisk until foamy; gradually add sugar, beating well 1 minute. Stir in milk, vanilla, salt, and breadcrumb mixture.

Pour mixture into a lightly greased 1¾-quart casserole. Bake at 350° for 45 to 50 minutes or until set. Serve pudding warm with whipped cream, if desired. Yield: 6 to 8 servings.

CHOCOLATE-ORANGE SOUFFLÉ ROLL

2 (4-ounce) packages sweet baking
  chocolate
⅓ cup water
1 teaspoon Grand Marnier or other
  orange-flavored liqueur
8 eggs, separated
1 cup sugar
2 tablespoons cocoa
1 cup whipping cream
3 tablespoons powdered sugar
½ teaspoon vanilla extract
  Additional powdered sugar
  Semisweet chocolate-dipped
  orange sections

Grease bottom and sides of an 18- x 12-
x 1-inch jellyroll pan with vegetable oil;
line with wax paper.

Combine chocolate and water in top of a
double boiler; bring water to a boil. Reduce
heat to low; cook, stirring occasionally,
until chocolate melts. Stir in Grand Marnier; set aside to cool.

Place egg yolks in a large bowl; beat at
high speed of an electric mixer until foamy.
Gradually add 1 cup sugar, beating until
thick and lemon colored. Gradually add
chocolate mixture, mixing well.

Beat egg whites (at room temperature)
at high speed of an electric mixer until stiff
peaks form. Fold whites into chocolate
mixture. Pour into jellyroll pan, spreading
evenly. Bake at 350° for 20 minutes. Immediately cover with a damp linen towel;
cool on a wire rack 20 minutes. Remove
towel. Loosen edges of soufflé with a metal
spatula; sift cocoa over top.

Place 2 lengths of wax paper (longer
than jellyroll pan) over soufflé. Holding
both ends of wax paper and pan, quickly
invert pan. Remove pan and carefully peel
paper from soufflé.

Beat whipping cream until foamy; gradually add 3 tablespoons powdered sugar and
vanilla, beating until soft peaks form.
Spoon whipped cream mixture evenly over
soufflé. Starting at short side, carefully roll
up jellyroll fashion, using wax paper to
support as you roll.

Carefully slide roll (on wax paper) onto a
plate, seam side down. Chill. Sift additional powdered sugar over roll. Garnish
with semisweet chocolate-dipped orange
sections. Trim away excess wax paper
around sides of roll. Yield: 12 servings.
Note: The chocolate roll is fragile and
may crack or break during rolling.

HOT CHOCOLATE SOUFFLÉ

1 teaspoon sugar
2 tablespoons butter or margarine
2 tablespoons all-purpose flour
¾ cup milk, scalded
  Pinch of salt
2 (1-ounce) squares unsweetened
  chocolate
½ cup sugar
2 tablespoons brewed coffee
3 egg yolks, beaten
½ teaspoon vanilla extract
4 egg whites
  Sweetened whipped cream
  Grated chocolate (optional)

Lightly butter bottom of a 1½-quart
soufflé dish; sprinkle with 1 teaspoon
sugar, and set aside.

Melt 2 tablespoons butter in a heavy
saucepan over low heat; add flour, stirring
until smooth. Cook 1 minute, stirring constantly. Gradually add milk; cook over medium heat, stirring constantly, until
thickened and bubbly. Stir in salt. Remove
from heat; set aside.

Combine 2 squares chocolate, ½ cup
sugar, and coffee in top of a double boiler;
bring water to a boil. Reduce heat to low;
cook until chocolate melts. Stir chocolate
mixture into sauce.

Gradually stir one-fourth of hot mixture
into yolks; add to remaining hot mixture,
stirring constantly. Stir in vanilla.

Beat egg whites (at room temperature)
at high speed of an electric mixer until stiff
peaks form. Gently fold into chocolate
mixture. Carefully spoon into prepared
soufflé dish. Bake at 350° for 50 minutes
or until puffed and set. Serve immediately
with whipped cream and grated chocolate,
if desired. Yield: 6 servings.

CHOCOLATE-MOCHA SOUFFLÉ ROLL

6 eggs, separated
½ cup sugar
½ cup cocoa
½ teaspoon vanilla extract
  Dash of salt
¼ cup sugar
  Powdered sugar
  Mocha Cream Filling

Grease a 15- x 10- x 1-inch jellyroll pan with vegetable oil, and line with wax paper. Grease wax paper lightly; set aside.

Place egg yolks in a large bowl, and beat at high speed of an electric mixer until foamy; gradually add ½ cup sugar, beating until mixture is thick and lemon colored. Add cocoa, vanilla, and salt; beat at low speed of an electric mixer until blended.

Beat egg whites (at room temperature) at high speed of an electric mixer until foamy. Gradually add ¼ cup sugar, 1 tablespoon at a time, beating until stiff peaks form. Fold egg whites into cocoa mixture. Spread batter evenly in prepared pan; bake at 375° for 15 minutes.

Sift powdered sugar in a 15- x 10-inch rectangle on a towel. When soufflé is done, immediately loosen from sides of pan, and turn out onto sugar. Peel off wax paper. Starting at long side, roll up soufflé and towel together; cool on a wire rack, seam side down.

Unroll and remove towel. Spread Mocha Cream Filling over soufflé, and reroll. Place on a serving plate, seam side down. Chill. Before serving, sift additional powdered sugar over roll. Yield: 10 servings.

Mocha Cream Filling:

1½ cups whipping cream
 ½ cup sifted powdered sugar
 ¼ cup cocoa
 2 teaspoons instant coffee granules
 1 teaspoon vanilla extract

Beat whipping cream until foamy; gradually add powdered sugar, cocoa, and coffee granules, beating until soft peaks form. Stir in vanilla. Yield: about 3¼ cups.

RUM-FLAVORED POTS DE CRÈME

8 (1-ounce) squares semisweet
   chocolate
2 cups half-and-half
1 tablespoon sugar
6 egg yolks, slightly beaten
2 tablespoons dark rum
  Whipped cream
  Slivered almonds, toasted

Combine chocolate, half-and-half, and sugar in top of a double boiler; bring water to a boil. Reduce heat; cook until chocolate melts. Gradually stir about one-fourth of chocolate mixture into yolks; add to remaining chocolate mixture, stirring well. Stir in dark rum.

Pour into serving dishes. Chill at least 8 hours. Garnish with whipped cream and almonds. Yield: 6 servings.

CHOCOLATE-RUM DESSERT

1 (6-ounce) package semisweet
   chocolate morsels
3 eggs, separated
2 tablespoons light rum
¼ teaspoon almond extract
¼ teaspoon ground nutmeg
  Whipped cream
  Chocolate curls

Place chocolate in top of a double boiler. Bring water to a boil; reduce heat to low. Cook until chocolate melts.

Beat egg yolks until thick and lemon colored. Gradually stir one-fourth of chocolate into yolks; add to remaining chocolate, stirring well. Remove from heat; stir in rum, almond extract, and nutmeg.

Beat egg whites (at room temperature) at high speed of an electric mixer until stiff peaks form; fold into chocolate mixture. Spoon into cordial glasses or demitasse cups. Chill. Garnish with whipped cream and chocolate curls. Yield: 4 servings.

CHOCOLATE-ALMOND VELVET

⅓ **cup chocolate syrup**
⅓ **cup sweetened condensed milk**
¼ **teaspoon vanilla extract**
1 **cup whipping cream, whipped**
¼ **cup toasted slivered almonds**

Combine chocolate syrup, condensed milk, and vanilla; chill. Fold whipped cream into chocolate mixture; pour into individual serving dishes. Sprinkle with almonds. Freeze 3 to 4 hours or until firm. Yield: 6 to 8 servings.

CHOCOLATE-ORANGE MOUSSE

2 **tablespoons light brown sugar**
½ **teaspoon grated orange rind**
1 **egg**
1 **egg yolk**
3 **(1-ounce) squares semisweet**
    chocolate, melted and cooled
1½ **tablespoons orange juice**
½ **cup whipping cream**
    Additional whipped cream
    Grated orange rind

Combine first 4 ingredients in container of an electric blender; process until foamy. Add chocolate, orange juice, and whipping cream; blend until smooth. Pour mixture into two individual dessert cups; chill 1 hour or until set. Garnish with whipped cream and grated orange rind. Yield: 2 servings.

AMARETTO-CHOCOLATE MOUSSE

1 **(6-ounce) package semisweet**
    chocolate morsels
18 **whole blanched almonds**
½ **cup amaretto or other**
    almond-flavored liqueur
2 **envelopes unflavored gelatin**
¼ **cup water**
4 **eggs, separated**
⅓ **cup sugar**
2 **cups milk**
2 **cups whipping cream, whipped**
2 **(3-ounce) packages ladyfingers,**
    split

Place chocolate in top of a double boiler; bring water to a boil. Reduce heat to low; cook until chocolate melts. Dip larger end of each almond into chocolate, and place on a wax paper-lined cookie sheet. Chill until chocolate is firm.

Gradually stir amaretto into remaining melted chocolate; set aside.

Combine gelatin and water in a medium saucepan. Beat egg yolks slightly; stir into gelatin mixture. Add sugar and milk, mixing well. Cook over low heat, stirring until slightly thickened. Remove from heat; stir in chocolate mixture. Chill until consistency of unbeaten egg white.

Beat egg whites (at room temperature) at high speed of an electric mixer until stiff peaks form. Set aside 1 cup whipped cream for garnish. Fold egg whites and remaining 3 cups whipped cream into chocolate mixture.

Line bottom and sides of a 9-inch springform pan with ladyfingers. Spoon chocolate mixture into pan. Cover and chill until firm.

Place dessert on a serving platter, and remove rim from pan. Garnish with remaining cup of whipped cream and chocolate-dipped almonds. Yield: 14 to 16 servings.

BLENDER CHOCOLATE MOUSSE

⅓ **cup hot coffee**
1 **(6-ounce) package semisweet**
    chocolate morsels
4 **eggs, separated**
2 **tablespoons crème de cacao**
    Whipped cream
    Sliced toasted almonds

Combine coffee and chocolate morsels in container of an electric blender; process until smooth. Add egg yolks and crème de cacao; process 1 minute.

Beat egg whites (at room temperature) at high speed of an electric mixer until stiff peaks form; fold in chocolate mixture. Spoon into stemmed glasses or individual serving dishes; chill until set. Garnish with whipped cream and almonds. Yield: 6 to 8 servings.

BRANDY-CHOCOLATE MOUSSE

1 (6-ounce) package semisweet
    chocolate morsels
¼ cup plus 1 tablespoon butter
4 eggs, separated
2 tablespoons brandy
¼ cup sifted powdered sugar
    Whipped cream (optional)

Combine chocolate and butter in top of a double boiler; bring water to a boil. Reduce heat to low; cook until chocolate melts. Remove from heat; stir in egg yolks, one at a time, beating well after each addition. Cool. Stir in brandy and sugar; beat well.

Beat egg whites (at room temperature) at high speed of an electric mixer until stiff peaks form; gently fold egg whites into chocolate mixture. Spoon into stemmed glasses, or individual serving dishes; chill until set. Garnish with whipped cream, if desired. Yield: 6 servings.

MOCHA ALASKA DESSERT

¾ cup vanilla wafer crumbs
¾ cup cinnamon graham cracker
    crumbs
½ cup finely chopped pecans
½ cup butter or margarine, melted
2 tablespoons cocoa
½ gallon coffee ice cream, softened
6 (1-1/16-ounce) English
    toffee-flavored candy bars,
    crushed
1 (7-ounce) jar marshmallow creme
1 tablespoon Kahlúa or other
    coffee-flavored liqueur
3 egg whites

Combine first 5 ingredients, mixing well. Press mixture evenly into bottom of a 9-inch square baking pan. Bake at 350° for 8 minutes. Cool.

Combine softened ice cream and crushed candy bars. Spoon over cooled crust; cover and freeze until firm.

Combine marshmallow creme and liqueur, mixing with a wire whisk until blended. Beat egg whites (at room temperature) at high speed of an electric mixer until foamy. Gradually add marshmallow creme mixture, 1 tablespoon at a time, beating until stiff peaks form. Spread meringue over top of ice cream mixture, making sure edges are sealed. Bake at 475° for 3 minutes or until lightly browned. Yield: 9 servings.

BROWNIE ALASKAS

1 (15.5-ounce) package fudge
    brownie mix
1½ pints strawberry ice cream
4 egg whites
½ cup sugar
    Candied red and green cherry
    wedges (optional)

Prepare brownie mix according to package directions using a 9-inch square baking pan; cool completely. Cut brownies into 3-inch squares.

Arrange brownies on a cookie sheet; top each with a scoop of ice cream. Freeze at least 1 hour.

Beat egg whites (at room temperature) at high speed of an electric mixer until foamy. Gradually add sugar, 1 tablespoon at a time, beating until stiff peaks form.

Remove ice cream-topped brownies from freezer. Spread meringue over ice cream, making sure edges are sealed. Bake at 500° for 2 to 3 minutes or until lightly browned. Garnish with cherries, if desired. Yield: 9 servings.

CHOCOLATE LADYFINGER
DESSERT

1 cup cocoa
½ cup sugar
4 eggs, separated
¼ cup water
½ cup butter or margarine, softened
1 cup sifted powdered sugar
1 teaspoon vanilla extract
½ cup chopped walnuts
2 tablespoons sugar
16 ladyfingers, split
1 cup whipping cream
1½ tablespoons powdered sugar
½ teaspoon vanilla extract

Combine cocoa and ½ cup sugar in top of a double boiler; mix well. Stir in egg yolks and ¼ cup water; bring water in bottom of double boiler to a boil. Reduce heat to low; cook, stirring constantly, for 5 minutes. Set aside to cool.

Cream butter, 1 cup powdered sugar, and 1 teaspoon vanilla in a large bowl; beat in cooled cocoa mixture until smooth. Stir in walnuts; set aside.

Beat egg whites (at room temperature) at high speed of an electric mixer until foamy; add 2 tablespoons sugar, beating until stiff peaks form. Fold egg white mixture into cocoa mixture; set aside.

Line bottom and sides of an 8-inch springform pan with ladyfingers, placing rounded sides of ladyfingers toward outside of pan. Spoon chocolate mixture into pan; cover and chill at least 8 hours.

Combine whipping cream, 1½ tablespoons powdered sugar, and ½ teaspoon vanilla; beat at medium speed of an electric mixer until stiff peaks form. Spread over chocolate mixture. Remove rim from springform pan. Yield: 6 to 8 servings.

FROZEN MOCHA DESSERT

- 2 (3-ounce) packages ladyfingers, split
- 1 cup water
- 1 tablespoon instant coffee granules
- 1 (16-ounce) package marshmallows
- 2 tablespoons cream sherry
- 3 cups whipping cream
- 2 (1-ounce) squares semisweet chocolate, grated

Line bottom and sides of a 10-inch springform pan with ladyfingers, placing rounded sides of ladyfingers toward outside of pan. Set aside.

Combine water and coffee in top of a double boiler; bring water to a boil. Reduce heat to low; add marshmallows, and cook until marshmallows melt. Remove from heat; add sherry. Set aside to cool.

Beat whipping cream until soft peaks form. Fold whipped cream into cooled

marshmallow mixture; pour into prepared pan. Cover and freeze at least 8 hours.

Place on a serving plate, and remove rim from springform pan. Top with grated chocolate. Yield: 14 to 16 servings.

CHOCOLATE DREAM DESSERT

- 2 dozen ladyfingers, split
- ¼ cup Kahlúa or other coffee-flavored liqueur
- 12 (1-ounce) squares semisweet chocolate
- 2 (8-ounce) packages cream cheese, softened
- ½ cup sugar
- 3 eggs, separated
- 2 teaspoons vanilla extract
- 2 cups whipping cream, whipped
- Sweetened whipped cream
- Chocolate curls
- Maraschino cherries

Line bottom and sides of a 9-inch springform pan with ladyfingers, placing rounded sides of ladyfingers toward outside of pan. Brush cut side of ladyfingers with Kahlúa. Set aside.

Place chocolate in top of a double boiler; bring water to a boil. Reduce heat to low; cook until chocolate melts. Cool.

Beat cream cheese and sugar at low speed of an electric mixer until light and fluffy. Add egg yolks, one at a time, beating well after each addition. Stir in melted chocolate and vanilla; mix until smooth.

Beat egg whites (at room temperature) at high speed of an electric mixer until stiff peaks form. Fold egg whites and whipped cream into chocolate mixture; pour into pan. Cover and chill at least 8 hours.

Place on a serving platter, and remove rim from springform pan. Garnish with whipped cream, chocolate curls, and cherries. Yield: 14 to 16 servings.

LAYERED ICE CREAM DESSERT

¾ cup chocolate wafer crumbs,
   divided
1 cup butter or margarine
2 (1-ounce) squares unsweetened
   chocolate
2 cups sifted powdered sugar
3 eggs, separated
1 cup coarsely chopped pecans
1 quart vanilla ice cream, softened

Sprinkle ½ cup chocolate crumbs in an ungreased 13- x 9- x 2-inch pan. Set aside.

Combine butter and chocolate in a heavy saucepan; cook over low heat until chocolate melts. Remove from heat. Add powdered sugar, beating 2 minutes at medium speed of an electric mixer. Add egg yolks, beating until smooth.

Beat egg whites (at room temperature) at high speed of an electric mixer until stiff peaks form; fold into chocolate mixture. Carefully spoon mixture over crumbs, and sprinkle with pecans. Cover and freeze until firm.

Spread ice cream evenly over pecan layer; sprinkle with remaining ¼ cup crumbs. Cover and freeze until firm. Yield: 15 servings.

CHOCOLATE-COFFEE FROZEN DESSERT

2 cups vanilla wafer crumbs,
   divided
¼ cup butter or margarine, melted
2½ (1-ounce) squares unsweetened
   chocolate
½ cup butter or margarine
2 cups sifted powdered sugar
1 teaspoon vanilla extract
3 eggs, separated
1 cup coarsely chopped pecans
2 quarts coffee ice cream, softened

Combine 1¾ cups vanilla wafer crumbs and ¼ cup melted butter, mixing well. Press mixture into a 13- x 9- x 2-inch pan; set aside.

Combine chocolate and ½ cup butter in a heavy saucepan; cook over low heat until chocolate melts. Remove from heat. Add powdered sugar and vanilla; beat 2 minutes at medium speed of an electric mixer. Add egg yolks, beating until smooth.

Beat egg whites (at room temperature) at high speed of an electric mixer until stiff peaks form; fold into chocolate mixture. Spread mixture over crumbs, and sprinkle with pecans. Cover and freeze until firm.

Spread ice cream over pecan layer; sprinkle with remaining ¼ cup crumbs. Cover and freeze at least 8 hours or until firm. Yield: 15 servings.

COOL CHOCOLATE-MINT DESSERT

½ cup butter or margarine
1 cup powdered sugar
2 egg yolks
2 (1-ounce) squares unsweetened
   chocolate
1 cup chopped pecans or walnuts,
   divided
2 egg whites, stiffly beaten
2 cups crushed chocolate sandwich
   cookies, divided
8 ounces hard peppermint candy,
   crushed
12 large marshmallows, cut in small
   pieces
1 cup whipping cream, whipped

Cream butter; gradually add sugar, beating at low speed of an electric mixer until light and fluffy. Add egg yolks, beating well. Place chocolate in top of a double boiler; bring water to a boil. Reduce heat to low and cook until chocolate melts. Gradually add chocolate to creamed mixture, beating constantly; stir in ½ cup pecans, and fold in egg whites.

Press 1 cup cookie crumbs into bottom of an 8-inch square dish; spread chocolate mixture over crumbs. Chill until firm.

Combine candy, marshmallows, remaining ½ cup pecans, and ½ cup cookie crumbs; stir well. Gently stir in whipped cream. Spread whipped cream mixture over chocolate layer; sprinkle remaining ½ cup cookie crumbs over top. Chill. Yield: 9 servings.

CHOCOLATE DREAM CRÊPES

½ cup semisweet chocolate morsels
2 tablespoons butter or margarine
½ cup sifted powdered sugar
¼ cup light corn syrup
2 tablespoons crème de cacao
2 tablespoons water
½ teaspoon vanilla extract
1 quart chocolate ice cream
Chocolate Crêpes
½ cup chopped pecans

Combine chocolate morsels and butter in top of a double boiler; bring water to a boil. Reduce heat to low; cook until chocolate melts. Remove from heat. Add powdered sugar, syrup, crème de cacao, water, and vanilla, stirring until smooth.

Spoon about 3 tablespoons ice cream down center of each Chocolate Crêpe; fold sides over, and place seam side down on serving dishes. Spoon warm chocolate sauce over each; sprinkle with chopped pecans. Yield: 10 servings.

Chocolate Crêpes:

½ cup all-purpose flour
1 tablespoon cocoa
2 teaspoons sugar
Dash of salt
¾ cup milk
¼ teaspoon almond extract
1 egg
2 teaspoons butter or margarine, melted
Vegetable oil

Combine flour, cocoa, sugar, and salt. Add milk and almond extract; beat at low speed of an electric mixer until smooth. Add egg, and beat well; stir in butter. Refrigerate batter 2 hours. (This allows flour particles to swell and soften so that crêpes are light in texture.)

Brush bottom of a 6-inch crêpe pan or heavy skillet with oil; place over medium heat until just hot, not smoking.

Pour 2 tablespoons batter into pan; quickly tilt pan in all directions so batter covers pan in a thin film. Cook 1 minute or until lightly browned.

Lift edge of crêpe to test for doneness. Crêpe is ready for flipping when it can be shaken loose from pan. Flip crêpe, and cook about 30 seconds on other side. (This side is rarely more than spotty brown and is the side on which the filling is placed.)

Place crêpes on a towel to cool. Stack between layers of wax paper to prevent sticking. Repeat until all batter is used. Yield: 10 (6-inch) crêpes.

MOCHA CHIFFON

1 envelope unflavored gelatin
¼ cup cold water
¾ cup milk
⅓ cup semisweet chocolate morsels
3 tablespoons cocoa
2 eggs, separated
½ cup sugar
2 teaspoons instant coffee granules
1 teaspoon vanilla extract
1 cup whipping cream, whipped
Additional whipped cream (optional)
Chocolate shavings (optional)

Sprinkle gelatin over water; let stand 5 minutes.

Combine milk, chocolate morsels, and cocoa in a heavy saucepan; cook over low heat until chocolate melts.

Combine egg yolks and sugar in a small mixing bowl, stirring well. Gradually stir about one-fourth of hot mixture into egg yolk mixture; add to remaining hot mixture, stirring constantly.

Add coffee granules to hot mixture. Cook over low heat, stirring constantly, until mixture thickens. Remove from heat and stir in softened gelatin and vanilla. Chill until mixture is consistency of unbeaten egg white.

Beat egg whites (at room temperature) at high speed of an electric mixer until stiff peaks form. Gently fold egg whites into coffee mixture.

Gently fold whipped cream into egg white mixture. Spoon into a 1-quart casserole, and chill until firm. Garnish with additional whipped cream and chocolate shavings, if desired. Yield: 4 to 6 servings.

ROYAL MOCHA FREEZE

1 pint whipping cream
1 (5.5-ounce) can chocolate syrup
⅓ cup brandy
1 quart coffee ice cream, softened
1 (6-ounce) package semisweet
    chocolate morsels
¾ cup chopped almonds, toasted
    Whipped cream (optional)
    Chocolate leaves (optional)
    Maraschino cherries (optional)

Combine whipping cream, chocolate syrup, and brandy; beat at low speed of an electric mixer until thickened. Place ice cream in a large plastic or metal freezer container; fold chocolate mixture into ice cream. Stir in chocolate morsels and almonds. Freeze, uncovered, about 3 hours. Remove from freezer, and stir well. Cover and freeze until firm.

Spoon into parfait glasses and garnish with whipped cream, chocolate leaves, and maraschino cherries, if desired. Yield: about 12 servings.

CHOCOLATE-MINT CUPS

2 (1-ounce) squares unsweetened
    chocolate, melted
1 cup butter, softened
2 cups powdered sugar
4 eggs
2 teaspoons vanilla extract
1 teaspoon peppermint extract
12 vanilla wafers, finely crushed
¼ cup finely chopped pecans

Place chocolate in a small, heavy saucepan; cook over low heat until chocolate melts. Set aside to cool.

Cream butter; gradually add sugar, beating at low speed of an electric mixer until light and fluffy. Add eggs, one at a time, beating well after each addition. Add chocolate and flavorings; mix well.

Combine vanilla wafer crumbs and pecans; stir well. Sprinkle half of crumb mixture into 12 ungreased muffin cups.

Spoon chocolate mixture over crumb mixture, and top with remaining crumb mixture. Cover and freeze until firm.

To serve, run a knife around edge of each muffin cup, and gently lift out dessert. Yield: 12 servings.

CHOCOLATE TORTE ROYALE

1 (6-ounce) package semisweet
    chocolate morsels
    Cinnamon Meringue Shell
2 egg yolks
¼ cup water
1 cup whipping cream
¼ teaspoon ground cinnamon
¼ cup sugar
    Additional whipped cream
    (optional)
    Whole pecans (optional)

Place chocolate morsels in top of a double boiler; bring water to a boil. Reduce heat to low; cook until chocolate melts. Cool slightly, and spread 2 tablespoons over bottom of meringue shell (layer will be thin).

Beat egg yolks until thick and lemon colored. Add remaining chocolate and ¼ cup water, beating until thoroughly blended. Cover and chill.

Beat 1 cup whipping cream and cinnamon at low speed of an electric mixer until foamy; gradually add sugar, beating until soft peaks form. Spread half of sweetened whipped cream in meringue shell. Fold remaining whipped cream into chocolate mixture; carefully spread over whipped cream layer. Chill at least 8 hours. Garnish with additional whipped cream and pecans, if desired. Yield: 8 servings.

Cinnamon Meringue Shell:

2 egg whites
½ teaspoon vinegar
¼ teaspoon salt
¼ teaspoon ground cinnamon
½ cup sugar

Beat egg whites (at room temperature), vinegar, salt, and cinnamon at high speed of an electric mixer 1 minute. Gradually add sugar, 1 tablespoon at a time, beating until stiff peaks form.

Spoon meringue onto unglazed brown paper. (Do not use recycled paper.) Use a spoon to shape meringue into a circle about 8 inches in diameter, swirling sides to about 1¾-inches high.

Bake at 275° for 1 hour. Turn off oven, and allow meringue to cool in oven 2 hours. Yield: one 8-inch meringue shell.

EASY ICE CREAM BALLS

½ gallon peppermint or vanilla ice
    cream
14 chocolate sandwich cookies,
    crushed
 2 (1-inch) squares semisweet
    chocolate
½ cup butter or margarine
 1 (5.33-ounce) can evaporated milk
 2 cups sifted powdered sugar
    Whipped cream (optional)
    Maraschino cherries (optional)

Scoop ice cream into 2½-inch balls. Lightly roll in cookie crumbs. Cover and freeze until firm.

Combine chocolate and butter in top of a double boiler; bring water to a boil. Reduce heat to low; cook until chocolate melts. Stir in milk and sugar. Cook, stirring constantly, until thickened and smooth.

Arrange ice cream balls in individual serving dishes. Garnish with whipped cream and cherries, if desired. Top with warm sauce just before serving. Yield: 18 ice cream balls.

CHOCOLATE CHUNK-PEANUT BUTTER ICE CREAM

 3 eggs
1½ cups sugar
 2 tablespoons peanut butter
 6 (2.16-ounce) chocolate-covered
    crispy peanut butter candy bars,
    crushed
 3 (13-ounce) cans evaporated milk
 3 cups milk

Beat eggs at high speed of an electric mixer; add sugar and peanut butter, beating well. Stir in candy bars and milk.

Pour mixture into freezer can of a 5-quart hand-turned or electric freezer. Freeze according to manufacturer's instructions. Ripen 1 hour. Yield: 1 gallon.

CHOCOLATE DESSERT SHELLS

⅔ cup semisweet chocolate morsels
2 cups flaked coconut
½ cup chopped pecans or walnuts
    Ice cream or fruit

Place chocolate morsels in a heavy saucepan; cook over low heat until chocolate melts. Stir in coconut and pecans.

Line a muffin tin with 8 paper baking cups. Spoon chocolate mixture into cups; press firmly on bottom and sides to form a shell. Chill until hardened.

To serve, gently peel paper cups from chocolate shells. Fill shells with ice cream or fruit. Yield: 8 servings.

Pies

CHOCOLATE MERINGUE PIE

1¼ cups sugar
½ cup cocoa
⅓ cup cornstarch
¼ teaspoon salt
3 cups milk
3 egg yolks
3 tablespoons butter or margarine
1½ teaspoons vanilla extract
1 baked 9-inch pastry shell
  Easy Cooked Meringue

Combine sugar, cocoa, cornstarch, and salt in a heavy saucepan, stirring well. Gradually add milk, stirring until blended. Cook over medium heat, stirring constantly, until mixture is thickened and bubbly; boil 1 minute, stirring constantly. Remove from heat.

Beat egg yolks until thick and lemon colored. Gradually stir about one-fourth of hot mixture into yolks; add to remaining hot mixture, stirring constantly. Cook over medium heat 2 minutes, stirring constantly. Remove from heat; stir in butter and vanilla. Immediately pour into pastry shell. Spread Easy Cooked Meringue over filling, sealing to edge of pastry. Bake at 425° for 5 to 7 minutes or until golden brown. Cool. Yield: one 9-inch pie.

Easy Cooked Meringue:

½ cup water
¼ cup plus 2 tablespoons sugar
1 tablespoon cornstarch
3 egg whites
  Dash of salt

Combine water, sugar, and cornstarch in a small saucepan; cook over medium heat, stirring constantly, until transparent and thickened. Beat egg whites (at room temperature) and salt at high speed of an electric mixer 1 minute. Gradually pour cooked mixture into egg whites, beating 3 minutes or until stiff peaks form. Yield: enough for one 9-inch pie.

EASY CHOCOLATE PIE

1 cup sugar
3 tablespoons cornstarch
  Dash of salt
2 cups milk
3 eggs, separated
1 (1-ounce) square unsweetened
  chocolate
1 tablespoon butter or margarine
1 teaspoon vanilla extract
1 baked 9-inch pastry shell
½ teaspoon cream of tartar
¼ cup plus 2 tablespoons sugar

Combine 1 cup sugar, cornstarch, and salt in a heavy saucepan; stir well.

Combine milk and egg yolks; beat with a wire whisk 1 to 2 minutes or until frothy. Gradually stir into sugar mixture, mixing well. Cook over medium heat, stirring constantly, until thickened and bubbly. Remove from heat; add chocolate, butter, and vanilla, stirring until chocolate and butter melt. Spoon into pastry shell; set aside.

Beat egg whites (at room temperature) and cream of tartar at high speed of an electric mixer 1 minute. Gradually add ¼ cup plus 2 tablespoons sugar, 1 tablespoon at a time, beating until stiff peaks form. Spread meringue over filling, sealing to edge of pastry. Bake at 350° for 10 to 12 minutes or until golden brown. Yield: one 9-inch pie.

CHOCOLATE CREAM PIE

1 cup sugar
¼ cup cocoa
¼ cup cornstarch
  Pinch of salt
3 cups milk
3 egg yolks
1¼ teaspoons vanilla extract
1 baked 9-inch pastry shell
½ cup whipping cream
3 tablespoons powdered sugar
¼ cup chopped almonds, toasted

Combine first 4 ingredients in a heavy saucepan. Combine milk and egg yolks; gradually stir into sugar mixture. Cook over medium heat, stirring constantly, until mixture becomes thickened and bubbly. Cook 1 minute, stirring constantly. Remove from heat; stir in vanilla. Immediately pour into pastry shell. Cover filling with wax paper. Cool 30 minutes; chill until firm.

Beat whipping cream at high speed of an electric mixer until foamy; gradually add powdered sugar, beating until soft peaks form. Spoon whipped cream around edge of pie; sprinkle with almonds. Yield: one 9-inch pie.

CHOCOLATE WHIPPED CREAM PIE

2 (1-ounce) squares unsweetened
  chocolate
¾ cup sugar
  Pinch of salt
¼ cup plus 1 tablespoon all-purpose
  flour
1 (13-ounce) can evaporated milk,
  divided
2 egg yolks, well beaten
1 cup water
2 cups miniature marshmallows
¼ cup butter or margarine
1 (9-inch) graham cracker crust
½ pint whipping cream
¼ cup sugar
  Grated unsweetened chocolate

Place chocolate in top of a double boiler; bring water to a boil. Reduce heat to low; cook until chocolate melts. Add ¾ cup sugar, salt, flour, and ⅓ cup evaporated milk, stirring well.

Add a small amount of chocolate mixture to egg yolks, mixing well; add to remaining hot mixture, stirring constantly. Stir in water and remaining evaporated milk. Cook over boiling water until smooth and thickened, stirring constantly. Remove from heat. Add marshmallows and butter, stirring until melted. Cool.

Pour filling into crust. Cover and chill thoroughly. Combine whipping cream and ¼ cup sugar; beat at high speed of an electric mixer until stiff peaks form. Spread over filling, and sprinkle with grated chocolate. Chill. Yield: one 9-inch pie.

CHOCOLATE CREAM PIE WITH CHERRY SAUCE

1½ cups whipping cream
 3 (1-ounce) squares unsweetened chocolate, coarsely chopped
¾ cup sugar
 2 tablespoons cornstarch
⅛ teaspoon salt
 2 eggs, beaten
1½ teaspoons vanilla extract
 1 unbaked 9-inch pastry shell
   Sifted powdered sugar (optional)
   Cherry Sauce

Combine whipping cream and chocolate in a heavy saucepan; cook over low heat, stirring constantly, until mixture is smooth. Set aside.

Combine sugar, cornstarch, and salt in a medium bowl, mixing well; stir in eggs, vanilla, and chocolate mixture. Pour into pastry shell. Bake at 400° for 35 minutes. Cool completely on a wire rack. Sprinkle with powdered sugar, if desired. Serve with Cherry Sauce. Yield: one 9-inch pie.

Cherry Sauce:

¼ cup brandy
 1 teaspoon cornstarch
 1 (16-ounce) can cherry pie filling

Combine brandy and cornstarch in a small saucepan, stirring until smooth; add pie filling. Cook over medium heat, stirring constantly, until thickened. Yield: about 2¼ cups.

CHOCOLATE-BERRY PIE

1¼ cups graham cracker crumbs
⅓ cup butter or margarine, melted
 3 tablespoons sugar
½ cup plus 2 tablespoons semisweet chocolate morsels, divided
 1 (8-ounce) package cream cheese, softened
¼ cup firmly packed brown sugar
½ teaspoon vanilla extract
 1 cup whipping cream, whipped
 1 pint fresh strawberries
 1 teaspoon shortening

Combine first 3 ingredients, mixing well; firmly press onto bottom and sides of a lightly greased 9-inch pieplate. Bake at 325° for 10 minutes. Cool completely.

Place ½ cup chocolate morsels in top of a double boiler; bring water to a boil. Reduce heat to low; cook until chocolate melts. Set aside to cool slightly.

Beat softened cream cheese at low speed of an electric mixer until light and fluffy; add brown sugar and vanilla, mixing well. Add cooled chocolate, stirring well. Fold whipped cream into cream cheese mixture; spoon into prepared crust. Chill at least 8 hours.

Set aside 1 strawberry; cut remaining strawberries into thick slices. Arrange slices over filling; place whole strawberry in center.

Combine remaining 2 tablespoons chocolate morsels and shortening in a small saucepan; cook over low heat until chocolate melts. Drizzle over strawberries. Yield: one 9-inch pie.

AMARETTO-CHOCOLATE CREAM PIE

 1 cup sugar
⅓ cup cornstarch
¼ teaspoon salt
 4 egg yolks
2¾ cups plus 2 tablespoons milk
 2 (1-ounce) squares unsweetened chocolate, chopped
¼ cup amaretto or other almond-flavored liqueur
 2 teaspoons vanilla extract
 1 9-inch baked pastry shell
 1 cup whipping cream
 1 tablespoon amaretto or other almond-flavored liqueur
¼ cup sifted powdered sugar
   Shaved chocolate (optional)

Combine sugar, cornstarch, salt, and egg yolks in a heavy saucepan; stir well. Gradually stir in milk; add chocolate. Cook over medium heat, stirring constantly, until chocolate melts and mixture is thickened and bubbly.

Remove from heat; stir in ¼ cup amaretto and vanilla. Pour into pastry shell. Place a piece of plastic wrap over filling; chill at least 8 hours.

Combine whipping cream, 1 tablespoon amaretto, and powdered sugar; beat at low speed of an electric mixer until soft peaks form. Spread whipped cream mixture over pie; garnish with shaved chocolate, if desired. Yield: one 9-inch pie.

KAHLÚA PIE

1 envelope unflavored gelatin
¼ cup water
2 (1-ounce) squares semisweet chocolate
½ cup sugar
¼ cup water
4 egg yolks
¼ cup Kahlúa or other coffee-flavored liqueur
2 egg whites
1¼ cups whipping cream
2 tablespoons powdered sugar
1 baked 9-inch pastry shell
Chopped toasted almonds

Sprinkle gelatin over ¼ cup water; set aside. Combine chocolate, ½ cup sugar, and ¼ cup water in top of a double boiler; bring water to a boil. Reduce heat to low; cook until chocolate melts.

Beat egg yolks until thick and lemon colored. Gradually stir about one-fourth of hot mixture into yolks; add to remaining hot mixture, stirring constantly. Cook, stirring constantly, until mixture thickens. Remove from heat, and gently stir in gelatin mixture and Kahlúa (mixture will be thin). Chill until slightly thickened.

Beat egg whites (at room temperature) at high speed of an electric mixer until soft peaks form; fold into chocolate mixture. Beat whipping cream until foamy; gradually add powdered sugar, beating until soft peaks form. Fold half of whipped cream into chocolate mixture. Spoon mixture into pastry shell; chill until firm. Top with remaining whipped cream; sprinkle with almonds. Yield: one 9-inch pie.

CHOCOLATE-ALMOND PIE

1 (7-ounce) milk chocolate with almonds candy bar
18 marshmallows
½ cup milk
1 cup whipping cream, whipped
1 baked 9-inch pastry shell

Combine candy bar, marshmallows, and milk in a heavy saucepan. Cook over low heat, stirring occasionally, until melted. Remove from heat; cool. Fold in whipped cream. Pour into pastry shell. Chill at least 8 hours. Yield: one 9-inch pie.

FRENCH SILK PIE

3 egg whites
¼ teaspoon cream of tartar
⅛ teaspoon salt
¾ cup sugar
½ cup chopped pecans
½ teaspoon vanilla extract
1 (4-ounce) bar sweet baking chocolate
3 tablespoons water
1 tablespoon brandy
2 cups whipping cream, divided
Grated sweet chocolate

Beat egg whites (at room temperature), cream of tartar, and salt at high speed of an electric mixer 1 minute. Gradually add sugar, 1 tablespoon at a time, beating until stiff peaks form. Fold in chopped pecans and vanilla.

Spoon meringue into a well-greased 9-inch pieplate. Using a spoon, shape meringue into a shell, swirling sides high. Bake at 300° for 1 hour. Cool.

Combine chocolate and water in a medium saucepan. Cook over low heat, stirring often, until chocolate melts. Cool; stir in brandy. Beat 1 cup whipping cream until stiff peaks form; fold into chocolate mixture. Pour into cooled meringue shell; chill at least 3 hours.

Beat remaining cup of whipping cream until stiff peaks form; spread evenly over top of pie. Garnish with grated chocolate. Yield: one 9-inch pie.

FREEZER MOUSSE PIE

½ cup butter or margarine, softened
¾ cup sugar
2 (1-ounce) squares unsweetened
   chocolate, melted and cooled
2 eggs
1 (4-ounce) carton frozen whipped
   topping, thawed
1 baked 9-inch pastry shell
   Whipped cream (optional)
   Shaved chocolate (optional)

Cream butter and sugar until light and fluffy; stir in chocolate. Add eggs, one at a time, beating at low speed of an electric mixer 5 minutes after each addition. Fold in whipped topping.

Spoon filling into pastry shell. Freeze until firm. Garnish with whipped cream and shaved chocolate, if desired. Yield: one 9-inch pie.

CHOCOLATE-MINT ICE CREAM PIE

20 chocolate sandwich cookies,
   crushed
¼ cup butter or margarine, softened
1 quart vanilla ice cream, softened
¼ cup plus 2 tablespoons green
   crème de menthe
2 tablespoons crème de cacao
1 cup whipping cream
2 tablespoons powdered sugar
   Chocolate shavings (optional)
   Chocolate curls (optional)

Combine chocolate cookie crumbs and butter, stirring well; press into a buttered 9-inch pieplate.

Combine ice cream, crème de menthe, and crème de cacao, stirring until smooth. Spread ice cream mixture evenly over crust; cover and freeze.

Beat whipping cream at high speed of an electric mixer until foamy; gradually add sugar, beating until soft peaks form. Spread whipped cream mixture over pie. Garnish with chocolate shavings and curls, if desired; freeze until firm.

Let stand at room temperature 5 minutes before serving. Yield: one 9-inch pie.

TIPSY MUD PIE

1 (15-ounce) package chocolate
   sandwich cookies, crushed
¼ cup plus 2 tablespoons butter or
   margarine, melted
1 banana, thinly sliced
1 tablespoon lemon juice
1 pint chocolate ice cream,
   softened
½ teaspoon vanilla extract
1 tablespoon instant coffee powder
1 (12-ounce) carton frozen whipped
   topping, thawed and divided
2 tablespoons brandy
2 tablespoons Kahlúa or other
   coffee-flavored liqueur
½ cup plus 2 tablespoons chopped
   pecans
2 tablespoons chocolate syrup

Combine cookie crumbs and butter, stirring well; press into a buttered 10-inch pieplate. Combine sliced banana and lemon juice, tossing gently; drain. Arrange banana in a single layer over chocolate crust. Cover and freeze until firm.

Combine ice cream, vanilla, coffee powder, ¼ cup whipped topping, brandy, Kahlúa, and ½ cup pecans, stirring well. Spread evenly over chocolate crust. Cover and freeze at least 8 hours.

Spread remaining whipped topping over pie; drizzle with chocolate syrup. Sprinkle with remaining 2 tablespoons pecans. Yield: one 10-inch pie.

FROZEN CHOCOLATE PIE

2 (4-ounce) bars sweet baking
   chocolate
4 eggs, separated
1 envelope unflavored gelatin
2 tablespoons water
1 teaspoon vanilla extract
   Dash of salt
1 cup sugar
2 cups whipping cream, whipped
1 cup chopped pecans
2 (9-inch) graham cracker crusts
2 tablespoons graham cracker
   crumbs, divided

Place chocolate in top of a double boiler; bring water to a boil. Reduce heat to low; cook until chocolate melts. Stir a small amount of chocolate into egg yolks; add yolk mixture to remaining chocolate, stirring constantly. Remove from heat.

Sprinkle gelatin over water; add to chocolate mixture, stirring until dissolved.

Beat egg whites (at room temperature), vanilla, and salt at high speed of an electric mixer 1 minute. Gradually add sugar, beating until stiff peaks form.

Fold meringue, whipped cream, and pecans into chocolate mixture; spoon equal portions into crusts. Sprinkle 1 tablespoon crumbs over each pie. Freeze 3 hours or until firm. To serve, let stand at room temperature 10 minutes before slicing. Yield: two 9-inch pies.

CHOCOLATE-PRALINE PIE

2 eggs
½ cup sugar
½ cup butter or margarine, melted
2 tablespoons praline liqueur
1 (6-ounce) package semisweet
    chocolate morsels
1 cup chopped pecans
1 unbaked 9-inch pastry shell
    Vanilla ice cream (optional)

Combine first 4 ingredients; beat at medium speed of an electric mixer until blended. Stir in chocolate morsels and pecans. Pour into pastry shell. Bake at 350° for 30 minutes. Serve with ice cream, if desired. Yield: one 9-inch pie.

NUTTY CHOCOLATE CHIP PIE

¼ cup plus 2 tablespoons butter or
    margarine, softened
1 cup sugar
1 teaspoon vanilla extract
2 eggs
½ cup all-purpose flour
1 (6-ounce) package semisweet
    chocolate morsels
¾ cup chopped pecans
½ cup flaked coconut
1 unbaked 9-inch pastry shell

Cream butter, sugar, and vanilla in a medium mixing bowl, beating at low speed of an electric mixer. Add eggs, and beat well. Stir in flour. Gradually stir in chocolate morsels, pecans, and coconut. Pour mixture into pastry shell. Bake at 350° for 35 to 40 minutes. Yield: one 9-inch pie.

CHOCOLATE-NUT CHESS PIE

1½ cups sugar
3½ tablespoons cocoa
    Pinch of salt
1 tablespoon all-purpose flour
1 tablespoon cornmeal
½ cup chopped pecans
3 eggs, beaten
½ cup milk
1 tablespoon vanilla extract
1 unbaked 9-inch pastry shell
    Sifted powdered sugar (optional)

Combine first 6 ingredients in a medium bowl; mix well. Combine eggs, milk, and vanilla; stir into sugar mixture, mixing well. Pour into pastry shell. Bake at 350° for 45 to 50 minutes or until set. Cool. Sift powdered sugar over pie, if desired. Yield: one 9-inch pie.

CHOCOLATE PECAN PIE

⅔ cup evaporated milk
2 tablespoons butter or margarine
1 (6-ounce) package semisweet
    chocolate morsels
2 eggs, beaten
1 cup sugar
2 tablespoons all-purpose flour
¼ teaspoon salt
1 teaspoon vanilla extract
1 cup chopped pecans
1 unbaked 9-inch pastry shell

Combine milk, butter, and chocolate morsels in a small saucepan; cook over low heat, stirring constantly, until chocolate melts. Remove from heat.

Combine eggs, sugar, flour, salt, vanilla, and pecans; stir in chocolate mixture. Pour into pastry shell. Bake at 375° for 35 to 40 minutes. Yield: one 9-inch pie.

Sauces and Frostings

CLASSIC CHOCOLATE SAUCE

- **2 (1-ounce) squares unsweetened chocolate**
- **¼ cup butter or margarine**
- **1¼ cups sugar**
- **½ teaspoon salt**
- **¾ cup evaporated milk**
- **½ teaspoon vanilla extract**

Place chocolate and butter in top of a double boiler; bring water to a boil. Reduce heat to low; cook until chocolate melts. Stir in sugar, salt, and milk. Cook over medium heat, stirring until sugar dissolves and sauce is smooth. Stir in vanilla. Serve warm over ice cream. Store in refrigerator. Yield: 2 cups.

BLENDER CHOCOLATE-CHERRY SAUCE

- **½ cup pitted fresh sweet cherries**
- **½ cup chocolate syrup**

Combine cherries and chocolate syrup in container of an electric blender; process 15 seconds at high speed. Serve over vanilla ice cream. Store in refrigerator. Yield: about 1 cup.

BEST FUDGE SAUCE

- **1 cup sugar**
- **2 tablespoons cocoa**
- **¼ cup milk**
- **¼ cup whipping cream**
- **2 tablespoons light corn syrup**
- **1 tablespoon butter or margarine**
- **½ tablespoon vanilla extract**

Combine sugar and cocoa; stir in milk. Add whipping cream, corn syrup, and butter; mix well. Cook over medium heat, stirring constantly, just until mixture comes to a boil. Reduce heat, and simmer 10 minutes without stirring. Remove from heat; stir in vanilla. Serve warm over ice cream. Store in refrigerator. Yield: 1 cup.

EASY HOT FUDGE SAUCE

3 tablespoons cocoa
1 cup sugar
1 (5.33-ounce) can evaporated milk
1 tablespoon butter or margarine
1 teaspoon vanilla extract

Combine cocoa and sugar in a small saucepan; stir in milk. Cook over low heat, stirring constantly, just until mixture comes to a boil. Remove from heat; add butter and vanilla, stirring until butter melts. Serve warm over ice cream. Store in refrigerator. Yield: 1⅓ cups.

QUICK HOT FUDGE SAUCE

1 cup sugar
⅓ cup cocoa
2 tablespoons all-purpose flour
¼ teaspoon salt
1 tablespoon butter or margarine
1 cup boiling water
1 teaspoon vanilla extract

Combine first 5 ingredients in a saucepan, stirring well. Gradually add water; cook over medium heat, stirring constantly, until smooth and thickened. Bring to a boil; boil 2 minutes. Stir in vanilla. Serve hot over cake or ice cream. Store in refrigerator. Yield: 1¼ cups.

HOT FUDGE SAUCE

4 (1-ounce) squares unsweetened chocolate
2 tablespoons butter or margarine
¾ cup boiling water
2 cups sugar
3 tablespoons light corn syrup
2 teaspoons vanilla extract

Combine chocolate, butter, and water in a heavy saucepan; cook over low heat until chocolate melts, stirring constantly. Add sugar and corn syrup, stirring well. Bring mixture to a boil; reduce heat, and simmer, uncovered, 7 minutes without stirring. Remove from heat, and stir in vanilla.
Serve warm over ice cream. Store in refrigerator. Yield: 2⅓ cups.

CINNAMON-FUDGE SAUCE

2 (1-ounce) squares unsweetened chocolate
1 tablespoon butter or margarine
⅓ cup boiling water
1 cup sugar
¼ teaspoon ground cinnamon
1 tablespoon corn syrup
1 teaspoon vanilla extract

Combine chocolate, butter, and water in a heavy saucepan; cook over low heat until chocolate melts, stirring constantly. Add sugar, cinnamon, and corn syrup, stirring well. Bring mixture to a boil; reduce heat, and simmer 7 minutes without stirring. Remove from heat, and stir in vanilla. Cool. Serve over cake or ice cream. Store in refrigerator. Yield: 1¼ cups.

CHOCOLATE-ORANGE SAUCE

½ cup whipping cream
1 (4-ounce) package sweet baking chocolate
½ teaspoon orange extract
¼ teaspoon grated orange rind

Place whipping cream in a heavy saucepan. Cook over low heat just until thoroughly heated (do not boil). Remove from heat. Add chocolate; stir until melted. Stir in orange extract and orange rind. Chill. Serve over ice cream. Store in refrigerator. Yield: ¾ cup.

OLD-FASHIONED CHOCOLATE SAUCE

1 cup sugar
¼ cup plus 1 tablespoon cocoa
3 tablespoons all-purpose flour
1 cup milk
2 tablespoons butter or margarine
1 teaspoon vanilla extract

Combine first 4 ingredients in a medium saucepan. Cook over medium heat, stirring constantly, until slightly thickened. Remove from heat, and stir in butter and vanilla. Serve warm over ice cream. Store in refrigerator. Yield: 2 cups.

HEAVENLY CHOCOLATE SAUCE

½ cup butter or margarine
4 (1-ounce) squares unsweetened
   chocolate
3 cups sugar
1 (13-ounce) can evaporated milk
½ teaspoon salt

Place butter and chocolate in top of a double boiler; bring water to a boil. Reduce heat to low; cook until chocolate melts. Stir in sugar, milk, and salt. Cook over medium heat, stirring constantly, until smooth. Serve warm over ice cream. Store in refrigerator. Yield: about 4 cups.

CHOCOLATE-PEANUT BUTTER SAUCE

1 (6-ounce) package semisweet
   chocolate morsels
¼ cup crunchy peanut butter
¼ cup light corn syrup
¼ cup plus 1 tablespoon whipping
   cream

Place chocolate morsels in top of a double boiler; bring water to a boil. Reduce heat to low; cook until chocolate melts. Add peanut butter, stirring until blended. Remove from heat, and stir in corn syrup and whipping cream. Serve warm over ice cream. Store in refrigerator. Yield: about 1¼ cups.

KAHLÚA-CHOCOLATE SAUCE

6 (1-ounce) squares semisweet
   chocolate
½ cup Kahlúa or other
   coffee-flavored liqueur
1 tablespoon powdered sugar

Place chocolate in top of a double boiler; bring water to a boil. Reduce heat to low; cook until chocolate melts. Remove from heat; gradually stir in Kahlúa and sugar, stirring until smooth. Cool; serve with fresh fruit or ice cream. Store in refrigerator. Yield: ¾ cup.

CHOCOLATE FONDUE SAUCE

1 (12-ounce) package semisweet
   chocolate morsels
½ cup half-and-half
½ cup sugar
1 teaspoon vanilla extract

Combine all ingredients in top of a double boiler; bring water to a boil. Reduce heat to low; cook until chocolate melts. Pour into fondue pot; place over fondue burner. Serve with fruit or cookies as dippers. Store in refrigerator. Yield: 2 cups.

CHOCOLATE FROSTING

2¾ cups sifted powdered sugar
¼ cup plus 1 tablespoon cocoa
¼ cup butter or margarine, melted
2 egg yolks
2 tablespoons milk
1 teaspoon vanilla extract
⅛ teaspoon salt

Combine all ingredients; beat at medium speed of an electric mixer until smooth and thick enough to spread. Yield: enough for one 1-layer cake.

QUICK FUDGE FROSTING

1 cup firmly packed brown sugar
3 tablespoons cocoa
3 tablespoons shortening
1 tablespoon butter or margarine
¼ teaspoon salt
⅓ cup milk
1½ cups sifted powdered sugar
1 teaspoon vanilla extract

Combine first 6 ingredients in a medium saucepan. Cook over medium heat, stirring constantly, until mixture comes to a boil. Boil 3 minutes, stirring constantly. Remove from heat; cool.

Add powdered sugar and vanilla; beat at medium speed of an electric mixer until smooth and thick enough to spread, adding a small amount of milk, if necessary. Spread immediately on cooled cake. Yield: enough for one 2-layer cake.

CREAMY CHOCOLATE FROSTING

¼ cup butter or margarine
2 (1-ounce) squares unsweetened
   chocolate
2 cups sifted powdered sugar
⅓ cup evaporated milk
   Pinch of salt
¼ teaspoon vanilla extract

Place butter and chocolate in top of a double boiler; bring water to a boil. Reduce heat to low; cook until chocolate melts. Add sugar, milk, and salt; beat at medium speed of an electric mixer until smooth and thick enough to spread. Stir in vanilla. Yield: enough for one 2-layer cake.

HONEY-CHOCOLATE FROSTING

3 tablespoons butter or margarine,
   softened
3 tablespoons cocoa
¾ teaspoon vanilla extract
1 cup sifted powdered sugar
1 tablespoon milk
1 tablespoon honey

Cream butter; add cocoa, beating well at low speed of an electric mixer. Add vanilla, sugar, milk, and honey; beat until smooth and thick enough to spread. Yield: enough for one 1-layer cake.

PROCESSOR CHOCOLATE FROSTING

½ cup butter or margarine, softened
4 cups sifted powdered sugar
¾ cup cocoa
½ cup evaporated milk
1 teaspoon Grand Marnier or other
   orange-flavored liqueur

Position knife blade in food processor bowl; add all ingredients in order listed. Top with cover; pulse 2 or 3 times. Process about 1 minute, scraping sides of processor bowl occasionally until smooth and thick enough to spread. Yield: enough for one 2-layer cake.

CHOCOLATE-ALMOND FROSTING

½ cup semisweet chocolate morsels
¼ cup milk
¼ cup plus 2 tablespoons butter
¼ to ½ teaspoon almond extract
1¼ cups sifted powdered sugar

Combine chocolate morsels, milk, and butter in a saucepan; cook over medium heat, stirring until chocolate melts. Remove from heat; add almond extract and powdered sugar, stirring well.
Set saucepan in ice; beat until frosting holds its shape and loses its gloss. If necessary, add a small amount of milk to make thick enough to spread. Yield: enough for 1 dozen cupcakes or one 1-layer cake.

CHOCOLATE FUDGE FROSTING

¼ cup butter or margarine, softened
⅓ cup light corn syrup
½ teaspoon vanilla extract
¼ teaspoon salt
½ cup cocoa
1 (16-ounce) package powdered
   sugar, sifted
2 to 3 tablespoons milk

Cream butter; add syrup, vanilla, salt, and cocoa, beating at medium speed of an electric mixer. Add sugar and milk alternately, beating until smooth and thick enough to spread. Yield: enough for one 2-layer cake.

CHOCOLATE GLAZE

2 tablespoons butter or margarine
1 (1-ounce) square unsweetened
   chocolate
1 cup sifted powdered sugar
2 tablespoons boiling water

Combine butter and chocolate in top of a double boiler; bring water to a boil. Reduce heat to low; cook until chocolate melts. Cool slightly. Add sugar and water; beat at low speed of an electric mixer until smooth enough to spoon over cake. Yield: enough for one tube or bundt cake.

Index